YALE LANGUAGE SERIES

hond ẏſ ʒeſceapod ʒnũme ʒeʒonʒen

WORD-HOARD

An Introduction to Old English Vocabulary

Stephen A. Barney

SECOND EDITION

Yale University Press   New Haven and London

Printed in the United States of America by
The Murray Printing Co., Westford, Mass.

Library of Congress Catalogue Card Number: 85–40501
International Standard Book Number: 0–300–03506–3

The paper in this book meets the guidelines for permanence
and durability of the Committee on Production Guidelines
for Book Longevity of the Council on Library Resources.

10   9   8   7   6   5   4   3   2   1

CONTENTS

INTRODUCTION

This <u>Word-Hoard</u> aims to help a beginning student to master the more ordinary vocabulary of Old English. The total vocabulary of Old English poetry, as preserved in the six volumes of the <u>Anglo-Saxon Poetic Records</u>, is something over eight thousand words, of which about sixty percent are compound words. But a student need learn only a quarter of this number of words to know the meanings of over ninety percent of the running words he will meet in reading <u>Beowulf</u>. This list is composed of about two thousand words—those which are most frequent in the poetry a student will read as he begins to learn OE language and literature.

But the first glance at a page of OE shows that even learning two thousand words is not the feat of memory which it may seem. Most of the words are compounds whose meanings are usually determinable from the meanings of the bases of which they are composed. Furthermore, many of the words are related to each other, and it is obvious that any systematic attempt to learn vocabulary will advance much more rapidly by associating related words. In this list I have gone farther than the obvious, and have grouped together all of the words which are etymologically related—even a number which are not very obvious—in order to assist the memory. Once it is known that æðele means "noble," it is not very hard to learn that æðeling means "nobleman," and it is still not <u>very</u> hard to see that ēðel "native land" is related, and shares in a sense of concern with ancestors, of genealogical pride. These connections ease the burden of learning "Old Anguish," and they can refine the student's sense of the connotations of words.

The 2000-odd words fall into 227 groups of related words. I have arranged these groups in descending order of frequency of all the words in each group. The number in parentheses at the end of each group is the total count of the appearances of the words of that group in the poems on which I have based this list. The learning of vocabulary, then, will focus on key words, those listed

in the "Key-Word Index to the Groups." An early, particu-
larly valuable exercise would be to learn these key words.
(The Anglo-Saxons, too, had something like a list of key
words: the names of the characters in the runic alphabet
[the fuþorc]. Those which are not of doubtful meaning: feoh
"cattle," ūr "aurochs," þorn "thorn," rād "journey," ġyfu
"gift," wynn "joy," hæġl "hail," nȳd "need," īs "ice,"
ġēr "year," ēoh "yew," siġel "sun," beorc "birch," eh
"horse," mann "man," lagu "water," Ing (the god), ēðel
"homeland," dæġ "day," āc "oak," æsc "ash," ȳr "yew bow,"
gār "spear," stān "stone.")

Another aid to the memory is the fact that many of
the OE words have relatives in other languages. Because
the most helpful language is Modern English, I have been
careful to include modern reflexes of OE words. "Modern"
here means "after 1500 A.D." Many of these Modern words
are no longer used, except perhaps in remote dialects
("taw, dree, wain, bairn, to worth"); nevertheless, most
of the Modern reflexes are still vaguely familiar, they
are interesting, and they can jog the memory. The "Key-
Word Index to the Groups" shows how very few of the
groups have no Modern reflex.

Among other related languages I have often given
the cognates of OE words which appear in Modern German,
Latin, and Greek. The German words are of course closest,
and students who know some German will have the easiest
time learning OE. The cognates in Latin and Greek are
much more obscure, and the connections between these
words are often less certain, in spite of the researches
that have been undertaken since Jacob Grimm in the early
nineteenth century formulated the pattern of relationships between the Germanic and the classical languages.
From the Latin cognates can come many mnemonic aids: for
example, the English word conceal derives ultimately from
the Latin celāre "to conceal." (If you know a Romance
language you can often use the Latin cognate even without
Latin or without a pair as easy as celāre/conceal.) The OE
cognate of celāre is helan "to conceal" (see No. 42).
The student will have to see that a Latin c often appears
in English as an h, if he wants to use this mnemonic aid,
but he might prefer remembering in this systematic way
to remembering by rote. And in this case he has another
aid: HELMet (which conceals the head) is related to
helan.

The texts on which I have based this list are those
most likely to be read by a student first encountering
OE poetry. I have used two splendid editions, whose
glossaries are also word-indexes of all the words which
occur in the texts (although neither editor acknowledges
the fact): John C. Pope, Seven Old English Poems (2nd
ed., New York, 1981) and Friedrich Klaeber, Beowulf

(Boston, 3rd ed. with 2 supps., 1950). The former contains the poems "Cædmon's Hymn," "The Battle of Brunanburh," "The Dream of the Rood," "The Battle of Maldon," "The Wanderer," "The Seafarer," and "Deor." Whether or not a student uses this particular edition, he will be likely to read most of these poems early on. Klaeber's edition also includes "The Fight at Finnsburg," but I have left this poem out of the reckoning. A frequency list based on these texts should represent fairly accurately the actual frequencies of words a beginning student will meet. Of course most of the words listed here are also common to OE prose. The vocabulary of this <u>Word-Hoard</u> is skewed toward the secular and martial in comparison with the whole corpus of OE poetry, but the religious texts are usually read later, and the peculiarly religious words are usually still obvious in ModE.

Omitted from the list are the forms of the verb "to be," the personal pronouns, the demonstrative pronoun/ definite article sē, sēo, þæt, and the words þe, þæt, and, on, in (and the relatives of on and in), nē, tō, þā. I have also not counted a few high-frequency affixes (e.g., a-, be-, ge-, for-, -līc, and -ig), but have always noted this omission in the comments on the group where each such affix would occur. Compound words, when they are composed of two bases each included in groups of high enough frequency to be numbered in this list, are counted twice. The list breaks off arbitrarily at a group frequency of twenty.

Two further warnings should be made. The definitions given of the OE words are brief notes, and by no means exhaustive: they define the words only as they are used in the poems I have selected, and even then they cannot register the complex nuances of many words. Also, note that the etymological groupings are of two different orders: some obvious, and some obscure and, even when firmly established, nevertheless conjectural. For instance, in No. 10 it is obvious that <u>winnan</u> "to fight" is related to <u>ge-winn</u> "battle"; but it is not so obvious (the relationship is much more distant) that <u>winnan</u> is related to <u>wynn</u> "joy." These more remote relationships are given partly because they are interesting; they are only given when authorities appear to agree on them. But surely the Anglo-Saxons would have sensed no connection between <u>wynn</u> and <u>winnan</u>; the recovery of the relationship is an affair of modern philology.

How this list is used will depend on the teacher. If the teacher has students memorize vocabulary, he might simply assign groups of words week by week, with omissions if he sees fit. Perhaps the first dozen or so groups could be skipped, because they are complex and include words of such high frequency that a student learns them

quickly simply by reading. Then perhaps twenty groups
per week, to finish the list in about eleven weeks. Note
that the highest frequency groups contain many of the
strong and preterite-present verbs--which after all preserved their unusual conjugations in OE (and ModE) because of their high frequency in speech.

Professor Pope's text has "normalized" spelling, to
make it easier for beginners with the language. His normalizations, not so extensive as those of Holthausen and
Magoun, seem to me to strike the right compromise for
beginners between the actual forms contained in the manu-
scripts (mainly ca. 1000 A.D.) and the "Early West Saxon"
dialect of OE reconstructed by grammarians. I have followed Pope's normalizations, except for words and compounds which appear in Beowulf but not in the poems edited
by Pope; these I have usually left in the original spelling (using frequency of spellings as a very rough guide
when there is a choice) except when it seemed pointlessly
unclear not to normalize slightly. The lists of compounds
under each group, therefore, contain spellings not seen in
the head-list of basic words. I have here and elsewhere
forgone rigid consistency for the sake of clarity.

The words in the head-lists are arranged according
to their importance and frequency, and according to the
obvious progressions of sounds (ablaut and umlaut) and
the grammatical forms which they present; here again consistency has not been the rule. The words are all identified as to part of speech: nouns by their gender alone,
verbs by their class alone, and the rest explicitly (adj.,
adv., prep., etc.). Strong, preterite-present, and
anomalous verbs, and weak verbs with unusual preterite
forms, show the "principal parts" after the infinitive
form. A number of less common words are enclosed in
brackets; teachers may wish to omit these from their as-
signments.

Strong verbs are identified with Arabic, weak with
Roman numerals. So [(ge-)healdan (ēo, ēo, ea) (7) "HOLD"]
indicates a strong verb healdan which occurs in our texts
both with and without the ge- prefix, without change of
meaning, of class 7, whose principal parts are healdan
(infinitive), hēold (1st and 3rd person, singular, preterite), hēoldon (plural, preterite), and healden (or ge-
healden) (past participle). The infinitives of preterite-
present verbs are followed by the forms for the first and
third person present singular, the second person present
singular, and the preterite singular (all indicative).

Nouns are identified as masculine, feminine, or neu-
ter, and as wk. (weak) if they are not strong. Weak
adjectives are also identified; if an adjective is used

as a noun, it is identified as sb. (substantive). Many
forms act as more than one part of speech; rather than re-
peat the form, I have the format [ǣr (adv., conj., prep.)
"before, ERE" (prefix) "ancient, EARly"]. This may be
read out: the word ǣr is found as adverb, conjunction, and
preposition, with the meaning (in all cases) of "before" or
"ere." The word is also used as a prefix, when it means
"ancient" or "early" (as ǣr-ġewinn "ancient strife"). Furthermore, the ModE words "ere" and "early" are derived from
this group. The words printed all or partly in capital
letters, then, are modern reflexes of the OE words in this
list. Note that the ModE word printed in capital letters is
not necessarily the direct descendent of the particular OE
form in question, but merely a descendent of its etymological group.

A slash [/] indicates alternate spellings of an OE
word which are important enough for one reason or another
to include. Parentheses are used to indicate parts of
words which sometimes, but not always, are joined to the
words in our texts. If a word has a ġe- prefix without
parentheses, then it always has the prefix in our texts
(but not necessarily in the whole corpus of OE). If a
ġe- prefixed word is consistently distinct in meaning from
its base word (a radical example is ġe-wītan, No. 52) I
have listed it separately. The numbers at the end of
each group indicate the frequency of that group's words
taken together. An asterisk [*] means that the following
word does not occur in any written document, but has been
reconstructed as a necessary ancestor-form of some word
by grammarians (e.g. PrimG and IE roots).

I have followed the usage of Pope and A Guide to Old
English (Bruce Mitchell and Fred C. Robinson, revised ed.,
Toronto and Buffalo, 1982) in the diacritical marks. A
small circle over a ċ or ġ means that the sounds were
palatalized, and are to be pronounced (according to modern convention) as the "ch" of "church" and the "y" of
"year." (The last sentence could have concluded with the
word "respectively"; here and elsewhere I omit it, letting
the reader assume that parallel lists are respectively
ordered.) Since sc and cg are always pronounced like "sh"
and the "j" of "judge" there is no need to mark them.
(In a few words, not in this list, like ascian, the sc is
pronounced like the "sk" of "asking.") The symbols [<]
and [>] mean that a form was "derived from" or is directly "reflected in" another form: [DAY< dæġ] means "day,
which is directly derived from the OE dæġ." I have put
macrons ("long marks") over long vowels, and over the
first vowel of long diphthongs (unlike Latin, there are
many short diphthongs in OE). Throughout, I spell the
voiceless th sound (as in "thin") with a thorn (þ), and
its voiced allophone (as in "then") with an eth (ð).

A hyphen [-] before or after a word indicates its
use as a suffix or prefix, or that a grammatical ending
has been omitted for purposes of illustration. Hyphen-
ated forms in head-lists indicate bases used only as
compounding elements in our texts; often these forms
will not have part-of-speech notations.

The terms "cognate," "kin to," and "relative to"
refer to etymological relationships, as far as I am
aware of the present state of philology. For etymologies I have relied mainly on Holthausen, Pokorny, and
the OED, but doubtless I sometimes fail to join what
ought to be joined, and join what ought not to be joined.
A cognate word is not necessarily immediately derived
from its kins in this list.

In the lists of compounds, a few important ones are
defined briefly when the meaning is not obvious from the
bases. The forms which are underlined are the most frequent compounds in the particular set of words (between
the semi-colons); I have underlined a compound only when
it occurs more than three times in our texts and is the
most frequent of the set: so [. . . ; eormen-, feorh-,
fīfel-, frum-, gum-, mon- "mankind," wyrm-cynn;] means
that among the seven compounds in our texts whose second
element is cynn "nation, kind," the most frequent is
mon-cynn which means "mankind."

On the important matter of word-formation--the
combinations of bases with affixes and the formation of
compounds--see Randolph Quirk and C. L. Wrenn, An Old
English Grammar (New York, 1958), Ch. IV; Jess B.
Bessinger, Jr., A Short Dictionary of Anglo-Saxon Poetry
. . . (Toronto, 1960), "Preface"; and Mitchell's Guide
mentioned above.

Works which I have found invaluable in preparing
this Word-Hoard are The Oxford English Dictionary;
F. Holthausen, Altenglisches etymologisches Wörterbuch
(Heidelberg, 1934, 1963); A. Campbell, Old English
Grammar (Oxford, 1959, 1964); J. B. Bessinger, Jr., and
Philip H. Smith, Jr., A Concordance to Beowulf (Ithaca,
1969); J. R. Clark Hall, A Concise Anglo-Saxon Diction-
ary, 4th ed. with supplement by Herbert D. Meritt
(Cambridge, England, 1894, 1962); J. Bosworth and
T. N. Toller, An Anglo-Saxon Dictionary (Oxford, 1882-
98) and its Supplement, ed. Toller (1908-21); Julius
Pokorny, Indogermanisches etymologisches Wörterbuch,
2 vols. (Bern and München, 1955-69).

I am deeply grateful to a number of friends and
colleagues for suggestions and corrections. Special
thanks to Ellen Wertheimer and David Stevens for their

great help with the first edition. Traugott Lawler has
supplied continual encouragement and correction. My
thanks also to Jeanne Andrew, Douglas Bradley, Mike
Morrison, and Jennifer Nomura for their help with this
revision

Irvine   S.A.B.
1985

ABBREVIATIONS

acc.	accusative	ModE	Modern English
adj.	adjective	ModG	Modern German
adv.	adverb	n.	neuter
anom.	anomalous	nom.	nominative
cf.	compare	OE	Old English
comp.	comparative	OED	Oxford English
conj.	conjunction		Dictionary
cpd(s).	compound(s)	"our texts"	the poems in Pope's
dat.	dative		OE _Poems_ and
dem.	demonstrative		_Beowulf_
e.g.	for example	pl.	plural
esp.	especially	ppl.	past participle
etym.	etymology,	prep.	preposition
	etymologically	pres.	present
f.	feminine	pret.	preterite
gen.	genitive	PrimG	Primitive Germanic
Gk.	Greek	pron.	pronoun
IE	Indo-European	rel.	relative
ind.	indicative	sb.	substantive
indef.	indefinite	Scand.	Scandinavian
interj.	interjection	sg.	singular
lang(s)	language(s)	Skt.	Sanskrit
Lat.	Latin	st.	strong
LWS	Late West Saxon	superl.	superlative
m.	masculine	vb.	verb
MidE	Middle English	wk.	weak

1.   þǣr (adv.) "THERE" (conj.) "where, if"; þonne
(adv.) "THEN" (conj.) "when" (after comp.) "THAN"; þanan
(adv.) "THENCE"; þēs, þēos, þis (m.,f.,n.) (dem. adj.,
pron.) "THIS"; þider (adv.) "THITHER"; þus (adv.) "THUS";
[þys-lĭč (adj.) "such"]; þenden (conj.) "while" (adv.)
"meanwhile."

These forms parallel the hw- forms of hwā, etc. (No. 3).
The highly frequent þæt, þē, þā are not counted in this
list: they would fall here. The initial þ- of this
group was unvoiced in OE, but (later spelled th) became
voiced by the time of ModE. The reflexes from this
group with voiced th- are rare sounds in initial position in ModE.   Phonologists have used the pair this'll/
thistle to demonstrate the contrast of voiced and unvoiced initial th-. The cognates of this "demonstrative
group" are omnipresent in the IE langs.: ModG da, der,
dann, denn, dieser "there, the, then, than, this"; Gk.
to "the"; Lat. is-te, tum, tunc, tam "he, then, then,
so," etc. ModE than and then were the same word in OE,
as ModG denn and dann were originally the same.
Cpd.: þǣr-on "therein." (399)

2.   swā (adv.) "SO" (conj.) "as"; swelč/swylč (pron.
dem., rel.) "SUCH (as)"; swelče/swylče (adv., conj.)
"also, as."

Cognate with ModG so, probably Gk. hōs, "as." The OED
has fifteen columns of discrimination of the meaning of
"so." Swelč (Gothic swaleiks) is derived from elements
meaning "so-formed" (swā-lĭč; cf. hwelč from hwā-lĭč).
The ModE SUCH derives from the rounded form swylč (a y
in OE often appears as u in MidE and ModE); the unrounded
swelč gives us dialect variants still heard, even in
U.S.A.: "sech, sich." (210)

3.   hwā, hwæt (pron. interrog., rel.) "WHO, WHAT"
(indef.) "someone, something"; hwæt! (interj.) "listen!";
for-hwon (adv., conj.) "WHY"; hwylč (pron. interrog.)
"WHICH" (indef.) "any(one)"; nāt-hwilč (pron. adj., sb.)
"someone"; hū (adv.,conj.) "HOW"; hwǣr (adv., conj.)

1

"WHERE"; hwonne (adv., conj.) "WHEN"; hwanan (adv.)
"WHENCE"; hwæðer (pron., adj.) "which of two, WHETHER";
hwæðer(e) (conj., adv.) "WHETHER, however, nevertheless";
hwider (adv., conj.) "WHITHER"; ǣǧðer (pron.) "EITHER";
ǣǧ-hwylċ (pron.) "each one"; [ǣǧ-hwā (pron.) "every one";
ǣǧ-hwǣr (adv.) "everywhere"]; ǧe-hwā (pron.) "each";
ǧe-hwæðer (adj.) "either"; ǧe-hwylċ (pron.) "each";
ǧe-hwǣr (adv.) "everywhere."

The compounds of the hwā group with ǧe- and ǣǧ- (see ēċe
No. 27) form indefinite prounouns, adverbs, and conjunc-
tions. It will be seen that the questions a journalist
is told to answer in his first paragraph are all cognate
words. The suffix -an of hwanan is the usual one to
indicate "place from which" (cf. foran No. 11, ufan
No. 9, norðan). Hwylċ (often hwelċ) was formed on roots
which correspond to hwā + līċ (see No. 167), "of what
shape." The instrumental of hwæt, hwī, gives us WHY,
not found in our texts but good OE. From ǣǧ-hwæðer
comes ǣǧðer, orig. ā + ǧe-hwæðer. This group, parallel
to the demonstrative group (No. 1), may be called the
interrogative group. The IE etymon of this hw- group
may be represented as *kw-, which appears often as p- in
Gk., and as qu- in Lat. (quis, quid, quo, cum < quum "who,
what, how/where, when/accompanying"). The German initial
w- yields ModG wer, wie, wenn, wann, welch, was, wo
"who, how, if, when, which, what, where," etc.
Cpds.: ō-hwǣr; nō-ðer (=nā hwæðer); wel-hwylċ. (201)

4.   of (prep.) "from, OF, out of"; æfter (prep.) "AFTER,
for, in accordance with" (adv.) "AFTERwards"; æftan
(adv.) "from behind"; eft (adv.) "again, afterwards, in
turn"; eafora (wk.m.) "son, heir" (pl.) "descendants,
retainers."

ModE off was separated from of after the OE period--
they were originally the same word--and new different
spellings and pronunciation distinguished them as adv.
and prep. The word has various and complex meanings as a
prefix (of-, æf-), among them as perfective, disjunctive,
and negative (e.g., æf-þunca "vexation, i.e. bad-thought,"
cf. "aversion"). Æfter is not "more aft" but "farther
off" (af + ter, not aft + er) in its historical development. Like for (No. 11), æfter is not used alone as a
conjunction in OE. Æftan derives from a form like Gothic
afta "behind," superl. of af "off." Cognate are Gk.
apo, Lat. ab, ModG ab "from." An eafora is one who comes
after.
Cpds.: æfter-cweðende; eft-cyme, -sīþ. (195)

5.　magan (mæ̊g, meaht, meahte) (pret.-pres.) "be able, can, MAY"; meaht/miht (f.) "MIGHT, power"; mihtig̊ (adj.) "MIGHTY"; mæg̊en (n.) "strength, MAIN, military forces."

The sense "may" for magan is the less likely; *mōtan (No. 101) usually is used for this meaning. The error is common because of the ModE derivative. The group is cognate with the Gk. mēchanē "contrivance" (hence our "machine") from mēchos "means." Main as in mainland and as in "the Spanish main" are from mæg̊en, presumably from the notion of a powerful expanse, of land or sea. Our verb MIGHT is from the pret. of magan, now used modally more often than temporally, as a mark of the subjunctive. The verb may not have been a pret.-pres. originally, but may have taken on the pret.-pres. forms by analogy with other vbs. The word mæg̊en is a special favorite in Beowulf.
Cpds.: æl-, fore-mihtig̊; ofer-mæg̊en; mæg̊en-āgende, -byrþen, -cræft, -ellen, -fultum, -ræs, -strengo, -wudu. (170)

6.　willan (wolde) (anom. vb.) "wish, be willing, WILL"; nyllan "will not"; willa (wk.m.) "desire, delight"; [wilnian (II) "desire, ask for"]; wĕl (adv.) "WELL, rightly, indeed"; wela (wk.m.) "WEALth"; [welig̊ (adj.) "WEALthy."]

Cognate are ModG wollen, Wahl, wohl "to wish, choice, well," and Lat. volo, nōlo "I wish (not)." The latter is composed like nyllan of a negative particle joined to the positive verb (ne + willan ⇒ nyllan); cf. nyt, nān, nis, nabban, etc. from wit, ān, is, habban, etc. From wille ic̆, nylle ic̆ "whether I wish to, or not" comes willy-nilly. OE (like all the Germanic langs.) has no formal future tense; in poetry, futurity is usually signalled by context (with the present tense form of the verb), and rarely by the ModE method of willan or sculan (No. 18) + infinitive (usually with some hint of the desire or obligation implied by the verbs). In MidE the word wealth was superfluously used along with the older word WEAL on the analogy of "health." Willan and wĕl reflect different ablaut grades of an IE root; the Gothic forms are wiljan and waila.
Cpds.: wĕl-hwylc̆, -þungen; wil-cuma, -g̊eofa, -g̊esīþ, -sīþ; ǣr-, burh-, eorþ-, hord-, māðð um-wela. (162)

7.　eal(l) (adj., sb.) "ALL" (adv.) "entirely"; ealles (gen. sg. as adv.) "completely"; nealles/nalles (ne + ealles) "not at all."

The ModE vowel a in ALL derives from the Mercian form
alle. The LWS dialect of our texts shows "breaking"
(diphthongization) of the æ, which comes from the Germanic a, to ea (pronounced æa), so *all > *æll > eall in
West Saxon. (It is assumed that all a's from PrimG were
changed to æ in OE if not followed by m or n.) In the
more northerly dialects (Anglian, which includes Mercian)
from which modern Standard English derives, *all > *æll
which "retracts" to all again. The rule is that before
h, u(w), l + consonant, and r + consonant, the vowel æ
breaks to ea in West Saxon. The word has no certain
cognates outside the Germanic langs. From eall + swā
comes "also," hence "as" (cf. ModG also, als). The gen.
pl. of eall is ealra, Anglian alra, whence MidE aller-,
alder- meaning "of all," and Shakespeare's alderliefest
"dearest of all." The use of the gen. sg. adverbially
in ealles is common; cf. our "nights" for "at night."
Cpds.: eal-fela, -g̊earo, -īren; æl-mihtig̊; al-walda
(an Anglian form). (159)

8.   man(n) (dat. sg., nom. pl. men) (m.) "MAN"; man
(indef. pron.) "one."

The i-umlauted vowels of the dat. sg. and nom./acc. pl.
reveal original case endings which contained an i. Mann
serves for both "adult male" and "human being (of either
sex)," in English; the other Germanic langs. adopted distinct words for the two senses: ModG Mann and Mensch
"human being." The latter form occurs in OE (not in our
texts) as mennisc (adj.) "human(s)," which survived to
the 12th c. The OE terms which discriminate sexes are
wer (Lat. vir) and wīf (+ man = woman). ModG, like OE,
has man in nom. (unstressed) meaning "one" (cf. French
on).
Cpds.: man-cynn, -drēam, -dryhten, -þwǣre; brim-,
ealdor-, fyrn-, glæd-, glēo-, gum-, hired-, iū-, lid-,
sǣ-, wǣpned-mann. (151)

9.   ofer (prep.) "OVER, above, across" (prefix) "exces-
sive"; [ufan (adv.) "from abOVE"; ufor (comp. adv.)
"further up"; ufera (comp. adj.) "later"]; up(p) (adv.)
"UP(wards)"; [uppe (adv.) "UP"; yppe (wk.f.) "raised
floor, high seat."]

Cognates Gk. hyper, Lat. super "above, beyond," ModG
über, ober, oben "over" and auf "upon."
Cpds.: ofer-cuman, -flēon, -flitan, -gān "pass over,"
-helmian, -hīgian, -hycgan, -hȳd, -mægen, -māððum, -mōd,
-sēcan, -sēon, -sittan, -swimman, -swȳðan, -weorpan;
upp-gang, -lang, -riht, -rodor. (151)

10. wynn (f.) "joy, delight"; (g̊e-)wunian (II) "dwell,
remain (with), inhabit"; wennan (I) "accustom (someone)
to, entertain"; wēn (f.) "expectation, hope"; wēnan (I)
"expect, suppose, WEEN, hope"; wine (m.) "friend,
friendly lord"; winnan (a,u,u) (3) "contend, fight";
g̊e-winnan (3) "WIN, achieve"; g̊e-winn (n.) "strife,
battle"; [wīscan (I) "WISH."]

The Lat. cognate venus "loveliness, Venus" probably gives
the original sense of the group, which combines love and
war. One takes delight (wynn, ModG Wonne) in a friend
(wine) to whom one is accustomed (wunian), and one has
great expectations for him (wēn), and may strive for him
(winnan). The ModE pair habit/habitation helps account
for the ideas of dwelling (ModG wohnen "to dwell")
and custom (ModG gewöhnen "to accustom") joined
in the group. ModG wünschen "to wish" preserves the n,
missing from wīscan. Winnan is connected with the group
as are connected the two senses of the Skt. cognate
vánati "desired, obtained." What is hope (wēn) in OE
has become merely delusion in the ModG cognate Wahn. The
word wine is easily confused with wīn (n.) "WINE" (the
beverage).
Cpds.: wynn-lēas, -sum; ēðel-, hord-, līf-, lyft-,
symbel-wynn; be-wennan; or-wēna; frēa-, frēo-, g̊eo-,
gold-, gūþ-, mǣg̊-wine; wine-dryhten, -g̊eōmor, -lēas,
-mǣg̊; ǣr-, fyrn-, ȳþ-g̊ewinn. (150)

11. for(e) (prep.) "FOR, beFORE, in place of" (as prefix, intensive, often destructive, perfective); fore
(adv.) "thereFORE"; forþ (adv.) "FORTH, away"; [g̊e-
forþian (II) "accomplish" (perfective of "to further")];
furður (adv.) "FURTHER"; [(g̊e-)fyrðran (I) "FURTHER,
impel"]; furðum (adv.) "recently, first"; foran (adv.)
"before"; forma (wk. superlative adj.) "FIRST"; fyrmest
(superl. adj.) "first, FOREMOST"; fruma (wk.m.) "beginning, chief."

The same root gives ModG für and vor, Gk. para, peri-,
Lat. prō-, prāe, per- (the last also a "perfective" prefix, like ModG "ver-"). Ultimately the pr- of Gk. prōto
and Lat. primus "first" is cognate. The use of for
alone as a conjunction does not occur in English before
the 12th c.; in OE for + þon, þȳ, þǣm, hwon, hwȳ (compounded or not) served as "therefore, because, wherefore,
why" etc. Note that the OE fyrst (frist) "a space of
time" (ModG Frist) is not a member of this group and
does not mean "first." ModE FIRST is derived from a
homophone fyr(e)st (ModG Fürst "prince") which would
fall here but does not occur in our texts. Like g̊e-,
for- as a prefix sometimes gives a verb a perfective
mood, indicating the completion of the action of a verb

(for-bærnan means "to burn up completely"). It also is
frequent as a first element in adverbial and conjunctive
compounds (e.g., for-þon). For- and fore- as compounding
elements or prefixes are not counted here.
Cpds.: æt-, be-foran; dæd-, hild-, land-, lēod-, ord-,
wīg̊-fruma; frum-cynn, -g̊ār, -sceaft "creation"; forþ-g̊eorn,
-g̊erīmed, -g̊esceaft, -g̊ewiten, -weg̊. (141)

12. beran (æ, ǣ, o) (4) "BEAR, bring, wear"; -berend
"bearing, having"; [-byrd (f.) "BURDEN, responsibility";
g̊e-byrd (f.) "fate"; g̊e-bǣran (I) "behave"; bǣr (f.)
"BIER"; byrele (m.) "cupbearer"; g̊e-boren (ppl. adj.)
"BORN, born together, brother"]; bearn (n.) "child,
BAIRN, son"; byre (m.) (1) "son, boy" (2) "opportunity";
[g̊e-byrdo (wk. f.) "child"; -bora (wk.m.) "bearer"]; bearm
(m.) "bosom, lap."

Related to Gk. pherō, Lat. fero "I carry." Presumably
one's bearm is where one carries things; a ship's bearm
is its hold. One's bearing is still an index of one's
behavior. ModE BIRTH is a reflex of byrd in a sense not
represented in our texts. Bearn is easily confused with
beorn (m.) "warrior."
Cpds.: æt- "bear away," for-, on-, oþ-beran; helm-,
sāwl-, reord-, g̊ār-berend; dryht-bearn; mund-byrd; bearn-
g̊ebyrdo; wǣg̊-bora. (141)

13. eald (adj.) "OLD"; ieldra (comp.) "older"; ieldesta
(superl.) "oldest"; [ealdian (II) "grow old"]; ieldu
(f.) "old age"; ieldu (m.pl.) "men (of old)"; [ieldan (I)
"delay"]; ealdor (m.) "chief, prince, ALDERman"; ealdor
(n.) "life."

The idea that an older man becomes a chief (ealdor) is obvious; for the idea that oldness and "life" (ealdor) are
connected, compare the words "age" and "aged," and the
word weorold (No. 99). Cognate are ModG alt, Alter "old
age" and Lat. alere "to nourish" (> alma mater "foster
mother"); hence the idea of eald is from an idea of grow-
ing up (Gothic and OE alan "to nourish, grow").
Cpds.: eald-fæder, -g̊eseg̊en, -g̊esīþ, -g̊estrēon, -g̊ewinna,
-g̊ewyrht, -hlāford, -metod, -sweord; ealdor "chief"
-lēas, -mann, -þeg̊n; ealdor "life" -bealu, -cearu, -dagas,
-g̊edāl, -g̊ewinna, -lang, -lēas. (131)

14. gōd (adj., sb.n.) "GOOD"; bet- (adv.) "better";
betera (comp. wk. adj.) "BETTER"; betst (superl. adj.)

"BEST"; bōt (f.) "remedy, reparation"; ğe-bētan (I)
"improve, remedy"; sēl (comp. adv.) "better"; sēlra/
sēlla (comp. wk. adj.) "better"; sēlest (superl. adj.)
"best"; sǣl (m.,f.) "time, occasion, happy time"; ğe-
sǣliğ (adj.) "prosperous, happy"; [ğe-sǣlan (I) "befall,
turn out favorably."]

The "gather" group (No. 162) may be related to gōd; if
so, the original idea would be "consent, suitability"
and hence goodness. The long vowel distinguishes it
from gŏd "God." The ModG cognate gut also has comp. and
superl. forms besser and best. These latter, and their
OE alternates sēlra and sēlest, are not etym. related to
gōd; they are degrees of other adjectives whose positive
degree no longer survived. The OE kins of betera and
sēlra, bōt and sǣl (cf. ModG Busse "penance," selig
"blessed, happy") suggest their original senses of reparation and prosperity. We still use "better" in the
sense of a mere return to a normal state ("It's all
better"). The word ğe-sǣliğ has shown a remarkable
history; from the notion of "blessed" still present in
ModG came in English a sense of "innocent," whence
"naive," whence SILLY. We use the reflex of bōt, BOOT,
in the phrase "to boot" meaning "in addition": "an
advantage" was taken as "something additional thrown in."
In Beowulf, sǣl is twice used with its synonymous rhyme-
word mǣl "suitable time" in happy formulas: "Þā wæs sǣl
ond mǣl" ("then was a time of joy"--l. 1008); "sē ğe-
weald hafað / sǣla ond mǣla" ("he [God] who has control
over times and seasons"--ll. 1610-11).
Cpds.: ǣr-gōd "antique and fine"; gōd-fremmend; bet-līċ;
weorold-ğesǣliğ. (129)

15. (ğe-)standan (stōd, stōdon, standen) (6) "STAND,
take a stand"; stede (m.) "place, position"; staðol (m.)
"foundation, firm position"; ğe-staðolian (II) "establish, confirm"; [stǣlan (=staðolian) (I) "establish,
impute, avenge"]; stellan (I) "place, establish";
[(ğe-)steall (m.,n.) "place, foundation, site"]; ğe-
stealla (wk.m.) "companion"; stǣl (m.) "place, position";
[stille (adj.) "steady, STILL"]; stōl (m.) "seat,
throne"; stefn (m.) (1) "prow, STEM of a ship" (2) "trunk
of a tree"; stefna (wk.m.) "STEM of ship"; [stefnettan
(II) "stand firm"]; stōw (f.) "place"; -steald (n., adj.)
"dwelling, situated"; [stæþ (n.) "bank, shore."]

This complex group, founded on an IE root *sta- and its
ablaut variants, is cognate with Lat. stāre, status,
sistere "to stand, status, to place (cause to stand)" and
the huge number of derivatives from these words (e.g.
estate, constitute, statute, stay, persist, stable,
stanza, establish, stationery); with Gk. stēnai, stasis,

stoa "to stand, stasis, pillared hall" (statics, ecstat-
ic, Stoic); with ModG stehen, Stand, stellen, Stamm,
Stall, Stuhl, Statt, verstehen, Stadt, Gestade "to stand,
position, to place, stem, stall, chair, place, to understand, town, shore"; and with words in all the IE langs.
except Armenian and Albanian. The reflex of stōl,
"STOOL," shows some degeneration of meaning. Stede and
stōw are places where one stands (often military); a
stæþ is a place to stand when disembarking from a boat.
Staðol and its derivatives have an important religious
connotation of security and heavenly confirmation. Stefn
has apparently unrelated homophones meaning "voice" (f.)
and "time, occasion" (m., like stefn "prow"); but the
variant of our stefn, stemn "prow" or "stern," reveals
its origin as the beam (tree-stem) to which the side
boards of a boat were attached, as in the nautical term
"from stem to stern." The compounds of ge-stealla rise
from a military sense of one's "taking a stand by another
person," being his "companion-in-arms." The present
tense (and ppl.) of the base verb has "n-infix" (cf. Lat.
vinco, vīci) not found in the preterite, so standan/stōd
(cf. wæcnan/wōc "waken") and ModE stand/stood.
Cpds.: ā-, æt-, be-, for-, wiþ-standan; bǣl-, burh-,
camp-, folc-, hēah-, mæðel-, wīc-, wong-stede; stede-fæst;
ā-, on-stellan; weall-steall; eaxl-, fyrd-, hand-, lind-,
nȳd-gestealla; brego-, ēðel-, gum-, gief-stōl; wæl-stōw
"place of slaughter, battlefield"; hæg-steald; in-
gesteald; bunden-, hringed-, wunden-stefna. (128)

16. mid (prep.) "with, together with, by means of"
(adv.) "in attendance, at the same time."

Completely lost from ModE (amid is not cognate in spite
of its sense) except possibly in midwife "with the woman"
even though mid was the regular word for our "with" (of
accompaniment). Cognates: ModG mit, Gk. meta-. (127)

17. ān (adj., pron.) "ONE, lone"; nān "not one, NO";
ān- "single, lone"; [ānunga (adv.) "entirely"; anga (wk.
adj.) "sole"]; (n)ænig (pron., adj.) "ANY, anyone, not
any"; [ænlīc (adj.) "unique, beautiful"]; āna (adv.)
"alone"; [ǣne (adv.) "once."]

The o of ModE "one" characteristically appears for a
West Saxon ā of our poetic texts (cf. stān "stone," hwā
"who"). The initial w sound of ModE "one," not spelled,
developed around the fifteenth century (still missing
from ONLY < ǣnlīc). Etym. related to Lat. ūnus, and
curiously to the words onion, ounce, inch, uncial,
eleven, atone. The high frequency of this group in the

elegies suggests their theme; āna in Beowulf esp. indicates heroic single-handed derring-do. Nān of course ⇒ ne
+ ān.
Cpds.: ān-feald, -floga, -genga, -haga, -pæþ, -tīd.
(124)

18. sculan (sceal, scealt, scolde) (pret.-pres.)
"SHOULD, ought to, must, SHALL"; scyldiǧ (adj.) "guilty."

The ModG cognate is sollen. The future sense "shall" of
sculan, most common in ModE, is rare in our texts; the
sense of obligation is dominant (see No. 6). Scyldiǧ is
related through an idea of debt: Gothic skula, ModG
Schuld "debt," hence "guilt." ModE "shilly-shally"
corresponds to shall I, shall I (not); cf. willy-nilly.
(124)

19. dryhten (m.) "lord, chief"; dryht (f.) "band of retainers, noble company"; dryht- "lordly, splendid";
drēogan (ēa, u, o) (2) "perform, undergo, endure."

The Gothic ga-drauhts "soldier" is related to the Gothic
driugan "to do military service"; hence the relation of
dryht and its chief the dryhten to drēogan. The idea of
suffering often felt in drēogan may well reflect its
early military sense as in the Gothic (cf. "drudge").
Like many old martial and royal terms, dryhten provided
Christian authors with a word for God. Drēogan survives
in the dialect phrase dree one's weird "endure one's
fate" (on weird see No. 23), but the important OE word
dryhten is lost in ModE.
Cpds.: frēa-, frēo-, gum-, mon- "liege lord," siǧe-,
wine-dryhten; engel-, mago-dryht; sibbe-ǧedryht; dryht-
bearn, -guma, -līč, -līče, -māðum, -scype, -sele, -sib;
ā-drēogan.   (117)

20. cyning (m.) "KING"; cyne- "royal"; cynn (n.)
"race, family, KINdred, KIND"; [ǧe-cynde (adj.) "innate,
natural"; cennan (I) "beget"; -cund (adj.) "deriving
from, KIND."]

Cognate with Lat. gens "race, family," genus "kind,"
(g)nātus "born," ModG Kind "child." Cyning derives
either from cynn "nation" + patronymic suffix -ing, or
from cyne- "royal" + -ing. Note the homophones cennan
(1) "beget" and (2) "make known" (No. 33). The cognate
relation of Lat. nātus to English cynn justifies the
frequent MidE translation of natura as kinde (hence

Shakespeare's "kind" = "natural, familial"). <u>Manna</u>
<u>cynn(es)</u> is a frequent formula.
Cpds.: beorn-, eorþ-, folc-, gūþ-, hēah-, lēod-, sǣ-,
sōþ-, þēod- "king of a people," worold-, wuldor-cyning;
cyning-bald, -wuldor; cyne-dōm, -rīċe; eormen-, feorh-,
fīfel-, frum-, gum-, <u>mon</u>- "mankind," wyrm-cynn;
ā-cennan; feorran-cund. (116)

21. <u>ǣr</u> (adv., conj., prep.) "before, ERE" (prefix)
"ancient, EARly"; <u>ǣr-þon</u> (conj.) "before"; <u>ǣror</u> (comp.
adv.) "before, earlier"; [<u>ǣrra</u> (comp. adj.) "former"];
<u>ǣrest</u> (superl. adv., adj.) "first, at the earliest."

The word <u>ǣr</u> is itself a comparative form, from *<u>airiz</u>
the comp. of *<u>air</u> "early." So <u>ǣror</u> and <u>ǣrra</u> are double
comparatives, the former composed in OE times, the lat-
ter in PrimG. ModE EARLY derives from *<u>ar</u> or <u>ǣr</u> + <u>līċe</u>.
The adv. <u>ǣr</u> is often used to give pluperfect force to a
preterite verb: <u>þæt hē ǣr ġespræc</u> means "what he had
said."
Cpds.: ǣr-dæġ, -fæder, -gōd, -ġestrēon, -wela,
-ġeweorc, -ġewinn. (114)

22. <u>habban</u> (hæfde) (III) "HAVE, hold"; -<u>hæbbend(e)</u>
"equipped with."

Whether the word is cognate with <u>hebban</u> "lift" (> HEAVE)
or Lat. <u>habēre</u> (or, more likely, <u>capere</u> "seize") is
disputed. Remarkable is the reduction of the verb, esp.
in its auxiliary use, from <u>habban</u> to <u>a</u> as in "He'd 'a
seen."
Cpds.: for-, wiþ-habban; bord-, lind-, rond-, searo-
hæbbend(e). (108)

23. (<u>ġe-</u>)weorðan (wearþ, wurdon, worden) (3) "become,
happen, (aux.) be"; -<u>weard</u> "(to-)WARD"; <u>wyrd</u> (f.) "fate,
WEIRD (personified)"; [<u>wierdan</u> (I) "injure, destroy."]

The verb survives in ModE in the phrase "wo worth the
day!" meaning "evil befall the day!" The IE root has
the idea "to turn," hence "turn into" > "become." So
the Lat. cognates are <u>vertere</u> "to turn" and <u>versus</u>
"furrow," or a "line" of verse, where the ox or pen
turns back. The OE auxiliary use of <u>weorðan</u> occurs as
well in ModG <u>werden</u>. The weird sisters of <u>Macbeth</u> are
the "fatal" or "destiny-knowing" ones; the Icelandic
<u>Urðr</u> (cognate with <u>wyrd</u>) is one of the Norns. The

variation of ð and d in the different forms of weorðan illustrates Verner's Law. (102)

24. gangan (ēo, ēo, a) (7) "go"; ģe-gangan (7) "reach, get, happen"; [gengan (I) "go"; gang (m.) "going, passage, flow"]; -genga (wk.m.) "goer"; [-genge (adj.) "going"]; gān (ēode) (anom. vb.) "GO"; ģe-gān (anom. vb.) "get, undertake, happen."

Gangan may be a lengthened form of gān, or gān may be a shortened form of gangan by analogy with standan, with its shortened alternate form in Germanic, ModG stehen. The ģe-forms of both verbs are good examples of "perfective" meanings. Cognate are ModG Gang and Gänger "passage, goer." The preterite of gān is from a separate verb ēode, otherwise lost, which may have been related to the Lat. īre "to go." The word ēode became yode in MidE, but 16th c. archaizing writers used yede. Cpds.: ā-gangan; be- "circuit, expanse," in-, upp-gang; ān-, in-, sǣ-genga; ūþ-genge; full-, ofer- "pass over," oþ-, ymb-gān. (101)

25. mōd (n.) "mind, heart, MOOD, high spirit"; mōdiģ (adj.) "bold, courageous"; [ģe-mēde (n.) "consent"; an-mēdla (wk.m.) "arrogance, pomp."]

The ModE derivatives mood, moody miss the powerful sense of mōd, as do the ModG cognates Mut, Gemut. Related to the (Doric) Gk. mōsthai "covet," perhaps Lat. mos "custom, will." Gothic mōþs means "anger, emotion." Cpds.: ǣwisc-, bolgen-, ēaþ-, ģalg-, ģeōmor-, gūþ-, hrēoh-, ofer-, sārig-, glæd-, stīþ-, swīþ-, wērig-, yrre-mōd; fela-mōdiģ; mōdiģ-līċe; mōd-cearu, -ċeariģ, -ģehyģd, -ģeþonc, -ģiōmor, -lufu, -sefa "mind, spirit," -þracu, -wlanc. (101)

26. (ģe-)dōn (dyde) (anom. vb.) "DO, perform"; dǣd (f.) "DEED"; dōm (m.) "judgement, reputation, glory, choice"; dēman (I) "judge, DEEM"; [dēmend (m.) "judge, God"; dǣdla (wk.m.) "doer."]

The IE root signifies "to place, set, put"--hence don and doff (do + on, do + off) refer to the placement of the hat. A thing established is a judgement, so our dōm (whose modern reflex DOOM has lost its sense of "judgement" in favor of a sense of the fate which impends, the finality of doomsday) is cognate with the Gk. themis "justice personified" via the IE root *dhē-:*dhō-. (These

12

conjectured IE forms show the "ablaut" of vowels in a
regular series of gradation which accounts for the quality of all vowels in IE, and is most visible to us in
the vowel gradations of the stems of strong verbs.) A
thesis (Gk.) likewise is a thing set down or proposed;
the Lat. cognates have the sense "put": abdere, con-
dere, dēdere "to put away, put together, give up." The
root may be the source of the dental suffix which forms
the pret. of Germanic weak verbs (cf. our modern DID +
infinitive = pret.). Dōm and dēman exhibit the effects
of i-umlaut.
Cpds.: dǣd-cēne, -fruma, -hata; ellen-, fyren-, lof-
dǣd; dōm-dæg̊, -g̊eorn, -lēas; cyne-, wīs-dōm; mān-for-
dǣdla. (99)

27. ēċe (adj.) "eternal" (adv.) "eternally"; ā, āwa
(adv.) "always"; nā/nō (adv.) "never, not at all";
ǣfre (adv.) "EVER"; nǣfre (adv.) "NEVER"; ǣg̊- (prefix
of indefinite generalization) "each, every, any."

The frequent word ēċe (esp. in the formula ēċe Dryhten)
is not used after the 13th c. It is formed on the root
(as in Gothic aiw) from which derive ā and āwa (and
ModG ewig "eternal"). Cognates are ModG je "ever,"
Gk. aiōn, Lat. aevum "lifetime, aeon." Less certain is
the relation of ǣfre to this group: it may represent
*ā-in-feore "ever in life," but this is admittedly
doubtful. The very common prefix ǣg̊- (see esp. the hwā
group No. 3) represents ā "always" + g̊e- (indefinite
prefix). The word g̊e-hwā means "each (one)," and
ǣg̊-hwā means "every one." Words with this prefix are
not counted in this group. A ModE reflex of the root
of ā is "ay(e)," (often in the phrase, for ay), some-
what archaic, which rhymes with "say" and is distinct
from "aye" meaning affirmative as a vote (homophone of
"eye"). (Strictly, "ay" is a Norse loan-word, itself
derived from the Germanic root from which ā springs.)
OE sōna "forthwith" and g̊ēna "further" perhaps contain
ā in unstressed form, but the words are not counted
here. (97)

28. fela (indeclinable pron.) "much (of)" (adv.)
"much"; full (adj.) "FULL (of)" (adv.) "wholly, FULLy,
very" (n.sb.) "(filled) cup, beaker" (prefix) "following, serving"; fyllu (wk.f.) "FILL, plenty, feast";
fultum (m.) "help, support"; [fylstan/ful-lǣstan (I)
"help"; folgian (II) (= full-gān, anom. vb.) "FOLLOW,
pursue"; folgoþ (m.) "position of service, FOLLOWing,
office."]

Fela was perhaps originally an adjective, from which the
adverb was derived (acc. sg. n.); the adverb took on a
substantive function, often with a genitive, but retains a
feature of adverbs, being "indeclinable," or showing no
variation of ending. Adverbs are also made from the gen.
(ealles) and dat. (ealle) of adjectives. The notion of
"service" in compounds of full appears to arise from a
sense of filling as satisfying, hence providing satisfac-
tory service (cf. "supplement" from Lat. plēre "to fill").
Ful-lǣstan and fulgān (in the form full-ēode) occur in our
texts; the forms fylstan and folgian may not have been rec-
ognized as identical: cf. stǣlan/staðolian (No. 15); wer/
weorold (No. 99). Likewise fultum is full + tēam (< tēon)
"service-provision": rarely in OE is it spelled fulteam.
Cognates in ModG are viel, voll, folgen "much, full, to
follow"; Gk. polys "much," plērēs "full" (whence pleroma,
the "fullness" of Gnostic and theological terminology);
Lat. plēre, plūs "to fill, more."
Cpds.: eal-fela; fela-fricgende, -ġeōmor, -hrōr, -mōdiġ;
eġes-, sorh-, weorþ-ful; medo-, sele-ful (as "beaker");
wæl-, wist-fyllu; mæġen-fultum. (97)

29. (ġe-)witan (wāt, wāst, wiste) (pret.-pres.) "know";
nytan "not know"; [bewitian (II) "watch"]; wita (wk.m.)
"wise man"; [(ġe-)witt (n.) "intelligence, senses"];
wītiġ, ġe-wittiġ (adj.) "wise"; wīs (adj.) "WISE"; wīse
(wk.f., and suffix) "manner, way"; ġe-wiss (adj.)
"trustworthy, certain"; wīsian (II) "guide, show the
way"; [wīsa (wk.m.) "leader."]

The archaic ModE verbs "to WIT, to WOT" and the ModE
noun WIT are obviously derived from this group. The
IE sense of the etymon is "see": "to have seen" is "to
know." So the cognates in Gk. are eidos "appearance"
(> idol) and idea "form"; in Lat. the important cognate
is vīdēre "to see," whence come many ModE derivatives.
Witan is related to wītan "blame," and ġe-wītan "go"
(No. 88), but the groups are separated in this list simply to avoid undue complexity. The translation of
wīsian, "guide," is itself a ModE word borrowed from
French, and the French word was borrowed from an early
German (Frankish) form of witan. ModG cognates are
wissen, Weise, weisen, Witz, gewiss, Gewissen "to know,
manner, to direct, witticism, certain, conscience."
Cpds.: nāt-hwylċ "someone (I know not who)"; ūp-, fyrn-,
rūn-wita; fyr-witt; wīs-dōm, -fæst, -hycgende; wis-līċ;
ġe-wis-līċe. (96)

30. līf (n.) "LIFE"; libban/lif(i)ġan (lifde) (III)
"LIVE"; lāf (f.) "LEAVings, what is LEFT as inheritance,
survivors"; lǣfan (I) "LEAVE."

The connection between leave and life, if the conjec-
ture is right, is in the idea of "remaining (alive)"
(see the Gk. cognate līparēs "persistent"); to leave is
to cause to remain. The IE root probably meant "to
smear, to be sticky." The ModG bleiben (be + līban)
"remain" and Leib "body" as well as leben "live" are
from the same root. In poetry the lāf of files or ham-
mers are swords.
Cpds.: edwīt-līf; līf-bysiğ, -dæğ, -frēa, -ğedāl,
-ğesceaft, -wraðu, -wynn; un-lıfiğende; ende-, eormen-,
here-, wēa-, yrfe-, ȳþ-lāf. (95)

31. wīğ (n.) "war, combat, martial power"; [wīgan (I)
"fight"; ğe-wegan (æ, ǣ, e) (5) "fight"]; wīğend (m.)
"warrior"; wiga (wk.m.) "warrior."

Cognate with Lat. vīci "I conquered." The word ğe-
wegan is distinct from its homophone wegan (5) "carry"
(No. 94). As often, a present participle (wīğend) has
been made into a noun (cf. friend, fiend--hence the e
follows the i). The group is lost entirely from ModE;
the mass of compounds show how easily these words came
to the minds of poets in search of the frequent initial w.
Cpds.: wīğ-bealu, -bill, -bord, -cræft, -cræftiğ,
-freca, -fruma, -ğetawa, -ğeweorðad, -gryre, -haga, -hea-
fola, -hēap, -heard, -hete, -hryre, -plega, -sigor,
-smiþ, -spēd, -weorðung; fēðe-wīğ; gār-wīğend; æsc-,
byrn-, gār-, gūþ-, lind-, rand-, scyld-wiga. (93)

32. cuman (ō, ō, u) (4) "COME, go"; [cuma (wk.m.) "vis-
itor"; cyme (m.) "coming, arrival."]

Often forms of cuman appear with w after the c, revealing
the connection with the IE root *gwem-. The Lat. venīre
"to come," cognate with cuman, shows the survival of
the w and the loss of the initial consonant in that
branch of the IE group. The o of the ModE spelling derives from the medieval spelling of o for u before
groups of "minims" (like the i-shaped strokes in u, m,
n) to avoid confusion--the spelling here indicates no
sound change (cf. monk for munk, both pronounced the
same). Our "become," from "be come," to have arrived,
has driven out weorðan "become." The ModE becoming
"apt, nice," is from this verb, but ModE "comely" is
from a separate root represented in OE cȳme "beautiful."
Cpds.: be-, ofer-cuman; cwealm-, wil-cuma; eft-cyme.
(90)

33. <u>cunnan</u> (cann, canst, cūðe) (pret.-pres.) "know, know how, be able, CAN"; <u>cūþ</u> (adj.) "known, familiar, COUTH"; [<u>cȳþþ</u> (f.) "known region, home"]; (<u>ġe-)cȳðan</u> (I) "make known, announce"; <u>cunnian</u> (II) "test, find out by experience, try"; <u>cennan</u> (I) "make known"; [(ġe-)cnāwan (ēo, ēo, ā) (7) "KNOW, recognize, perceive"]; <u>cēne</u> (adj.) "bold, KEEN"; <u>fracod/forcūþ</u> (adj.) "wicked"; [<u>on-cȳþþ</u> (f.) "grief."]

The present of <u>cunnan</u> was formed on the preterite of a verb meaning "to learn"; "to have learned" is "to know." Hence the pret.-pres. form; a new pret., signalled by the dental <u>ð</u>,was formed on the old strong preterite. The group is related to Lat. <u>(co)gnōscere</u> "to be acquainted," <u>nōvī</u> "I know" (itself a pret.-pres. verb: to have been acquainted is to know). The ModE pret. of <u>can</u>, <u>could</u>, includes its <u>l</u> by analogy with <u>should</u> and <u>would</u>, which have <u>l</u> historically (<u>scolde</u>, <u>wolde</u>). The loss of the <u>n</u> before the <u>ð</u> of <u>cūðe</u> is characteristic of OE and its most closely related langs., Old Saxon and Old Frisian, in the West Germanic Group. So we have <u>tooth</u> instead of *<u>tonth</u> for the ModE cognate of the Lat. stem <u>dent-</u>, and we have <u>mouth</u> instead of something like the ModG Mund "mouth." ModE <u>con</u> "to learn" was distinguished from <u>can</u> "to be able" in the MidE period. One's native land is where one's dear ones are, one's KITH (from <u>cȳþþ</u>) as in "kith and kin." KEN, CUNNING, CANNY also derive from this group, and the term <u>kenning</u> (from Icelandic). The relation of <u>cēne</u> to this group is uncertain (PrimG *<u>konj-</u>). To be intensely uncouth is to be <u>forcūþ</u>. The <u>cunnan</u> group may be related to the <u>cyning</u> group (No. 20); if so, <u>kith</u> is cognate with <u>kin</u>. Note <u>cennan</u> "make known" has the homophone <u>cennan</u> "beget." Also note the sometimes confusing forms of the verbs <u>cunnan</u> and <u>cunnian</u>. Cpds.: cūþ-līċe; <u>un-cūþ</u>, <u>wīd-cūþ</u> "famous"; ā-cȳðan; dǣd-, gār-cēne; feor-cȳþþ; un-forcūþ. (<u>Un-cūþ</u> and <u>wīd-cūþ</u> occur five times each.) (90)

34. <u>magu/mago</u> (m.) "son, young man" (prefix) "youthful"; <u>maga</u> (wk.m.) "son, young man"; <u>mæcg/mecg</u> (m.) "man"; <u>mǣg</u> (pl. māgas) (m.,f.) "kinsman (kinswoman)"; [mǣgþ (f.) "MAIDen, woman"; <u>māge</u> (wk.f.) "kinswoman"]; <u>mǣgþ</u> (f.) "tribe, nation."

The ModG cognate is <u>Magd</u> "maidservant." The very frequent <u>mǣg</u> often means little more than "man." It is remarkable that so important a word as <u>mǣg</u> was driven out of English by "kin" and the less punchy "relative." Cpds.: magu-driht, -rinc, -þeġn; hilde-, ōret-, wræc-mecg; cnēo-, fæderen-, frēo-, hēafod-, hlēo-, <u>wine-mǣg</u> "friendly kinsman"; mǣg-burg, -wine. (89)

35. sīþ (m.) "journey, venture, exploit" or "time, occasion"; ge-sīþ (m.) "companion, retainer"; sīðian (II) "journey"; sendan (I) "SEND."

The verbs sīðian and sendan are related as "to go" and "to cause to go," i.e. SEND (ModG senden). The senses of the group are joined in a phrase like "go and have an interesting time." Probably related to the Lat. sentīre "to feel," by a metaphorical extension of the sense. Apparently not related to the adverb sīþ "later" and its derivatives. Cpds.: sīþ-fæt, -from; bealu-, cear-, eft-, ellor-, gryre-, sǣ-, wil-, wrǣc-sīþ; for-sīðian; eald-, wil-gesīþ; on- "send (away)," for-sendan. (89)

36. sīþ (comp. adv.) "later"; sīðest (superl. adj.) "latest"; siþþan (adv.) "afterwards, SINCE" (conj.) "SINCE, after, as soon as, from the time when."

ModE "since" is a reduction of MidE sithence ⟨ siþþan. Cognate are ModG seit "since" and perhaps Lat. sērus "late." (89)

37. feorh (n.,m.) "life, soul, person"; fīras (m.pl.) "human beings"; ferhþ (m.,n.) "spirit, heart, time."

Feorh is a favorite compounding-element in Beowulf. The noun fīras is derived from feorh, whose nom. and acc. pl. form is feorh. To get at a feorh in a military context is to cut to the quick, the part of a person which makes him alive (or as we say, inversely, makes him mortal). Wīdeferhþ means "for a long time"; for the association of "life" with "time" see weorold (No. 99), ǣfre (No. 27), eald (No. 13).
Cpds.: geogoþ-feorh; feorh-bealu "mortal affliction," -benn, -bold, -bona, -cynn, -genīþla "mortal foe," -hūs, -lāst, -legu, -sēoc, -sweng, -wund; collen-, sārig-, swīþ- "stout-hearted," wīde-ferhþ; ferhþ-frec, -genīþla, -loca. (88)

38. lēod (m.) "man" (pl.) lēode "people"; lēod (f.) "people, nation."

Cognate with ModG Leute "people," Gk. eleytheros, Lat. līber "free." The synonymous and rhyming OE word þēod (No. 52) may have influenced the forms and sense of lēod. From lēod comes a noun lēoden "language" (cf. ge-þēod [and Deutsch] "language" from þēod "people") which survived into MidE, and was confused with the OE word lǣdđn from the word "Latin," the language of the

learned. Lēod is a favorite in Beowulf, often making a
verse with a national name in the gen. pl. ("Wedera lēode"
--1.225).
Cpds.: lēod-bealo, -burg, -cyning, -fruma, -g̊ebyrgea,
-hryre, -sceaða, -scipe. (87)

39. gūþ (f.) "war, battle, fight."

Obviously an important compounding element, but without
relatives in OE, or any descendents in ModE; the word may
be related to Gk. thoneys "murder," Lat. dēfendere "to
defend." Gūþ is not used as the second element of any
compound. Twenty-two of the gūþ compounds are unique to
Beowulf. The word is found in poetry only; words of this
wort must have given the poetry a special, perhaps archaic
quality hard to imitate in ModE without quaintness.
Cpds.: gūþ-beorn, -bill,-byrne, -cearu, -cræft, -cyning,
-dēaþ, -floga, -freca, -fremmend, -g̊etawa, -g̊ewǣde,
-g̊eweorc, -hafoc, -helm, -horn, -hrēþ, -lēoþ, -mōd,
-plega, -rǣs, -rēow, -rinc, -rōf, -scear, -sceaða,
-searo, -sele, -sweord, -wērig̊, -wiga, -wine. (Underlined cpds. each occur 6 times.) (86)

40. æt (prep.) "AT, in, by" (prefix) "with, at."

Cognate with Lat. ad "to, at." ModG zu (with bei and an
drove out "at." The cpds. with æt- are not counted
here. (85)

41. mīn (possessive adj.) "MY, MINE."

Like the other possessive adjs. (þīn, ūre, ēower, uncer,
incer, sīn), mīn is formed on the genitive of the personal pron. ic̊ (not counted in this list) and differs
from it only in taking adjectival endings in agreement
with its noun. (85)

42. helm (m.) "HELMet, protection"; ofer-helmian (II)
"over-hang, overshadow"; [be-helan (æ, ǣ, o) (4) "conceal, hide, cover"; heolstor (m.) "hiding place, darkness"; hell (f.) "HELL"]; heal(l) (f.) "HALL"; [g̊e-hola
(wk.m.) "protector."]

The root means "to conceal," especially by covering
over: cognate with Gk. kalyptein "to conceal" (whence
Apocalypse, "the unveiling") and Lat. cēlāre, occulere

"to hide," <u>clandestīnus</u>, and <u>cella</u> "cell, room." Gk.
and Lat. <u>k</u> often appear in OE as <u>h</u> (centum/hundred;
<u>canis/hound</u>; capere/<u>h</u>eave, etc.) as described in Grimm's
Law. HALL, HELL, HELM are all covered places of a sort;
derived from the same root are HOLE, HOLLOW, HULL, and
HOLSTER. <u>Helmet</u> is the Old French diminutive of <u>helm</u>,
which the French borrowed from German. ModG cognates
are <u>hehlen</u>, <u>Höhle</u>, <u>Hölle</u>, <u>Helm</u>, <u>Halle</u>, <u>Hülle</u> "to conceal, cave, hell, helmet, hall, cover."
Cpds.: grīm-, gūþ-, niht-, scadu-helm; helm-berend;
hell-bend, -rūne, -scaða; heal-ærn, -gamen, -reced,
-sittend, -þeg̊n, -wudu; g̊if-, medu-heal. (82)

43. g̊iefan (ea, ēa, ie) (5) "GIVE"; g̊iefa (wk.m.)
"GIVER"; g̊iefu, -g̊ieft (f.) "GIFT"; g̊iefeðe (adj.) "GIVEN,
allotted" (sb.n.) "fate"; gafol (n.) "tribute."

The frequency of this group in our texts is largely a
result of the aristocratic practice of gift-giving, by
lord to retainers, as the polite means of maintaining a
<u>dryht</u> in an amicable spirit of martial zest. A lord is
pre-eminently a <u>bēag-g̊iefa</u>. <u>Gafol</u>, on the other hand,
the method of buying off Norse invaders, is a term of
contempt--not found in <u>Beowulf</u>, which may have been composed before the Viking raiders struck England. The
idea of the <u>g̊iefeðe</u>, the donnée or pre-destined, constitutes part of the apparently fatalistic ideology of
the Germanic peoples before the full reception of Judeo-
Christian providential thought (cf. <u>wyrd</u> No. 23). The
word <u>g̊iefan</u> may be related to Lat. <u>habēre</u> "to have," and
hence <u>dēbēre</u> "to owe" (< <u>dē</u> + <u>habēre</u>).
Cpds.: ā-, æt-, <u>for-</u> "give," of-g̊iefan "give up"; bēag-,
gold-, māðum-, sinc-g̊ifa "treasure giver"; māðum-,
sweord-g̊iefu; fēoh-g̊ieft; g̊ief-heal, -sceat. -stōl;
un-g̊iefeðe. (81)

44. (g̊e-)sēc̊an (sōhte) (I) "SEEK, go to, visit, attack";
sacan (ō, ō, a) (6) "fight"; sacu (f.) "strife"; sæc̊c̊
(f.) "battle"; g̊e-saca (wk.m.) "adversary"; "adversary"
[sōcn (f.) "persecution, visitation."]

To seek out with a vengeance is to fight. The Lat. cognate <u>sāgīre</u> means "to perceive by scent"; to be sagacious
(< Lat. <u>sagax</u>) is to have a nose for the truth (as to be
sapient is to be tasteful--Lat. <u>sapor</u> "taste"). ModG
<u>suchen</u>, <u>besuchen</u> "seek, visit"; the Gk. cognate <u>hēgeomai</u>
"lead" gives us "exegesis," guidance out (of perplexity),
i.e. interpretation. The old sense of <u>sacu</u> as a <u>legal</u>
strife developed in meaning as a "cause," hence ModE
SAKE. The ModG <u>Sache</u> "thing" is from the same root;

there the semantic development was from a court affair
to an affair in general, a thing (cf. "thing" and Lat.
res "affair of law, thing," and the semantic development
of the Lat. causa "lawsuit" to Italian cosa, French
chose "thing." In Icelandic, the þing is the Parliament;
in OE a þing can be a judicial assembly as well as a
THING.) ModE "beseech" keeps the palatalized pronunciation of the ċ of sēċan. The infinitive shows i-umlaut;
the preterite forms retained the original ō (cf. þenċan/
þōhte, þynċan/þūhte, wyrcan/worhte "think, seem, work").
Cpds.: ofer-, on-sēċan; on-sacan; and-saca. (81)

45. (ġe-)healdan (ēo, ēo, ea) (7) "HOLD, keep, rule";
[ġe-hyld (n.) "protection."]

The ModE beholden "obliged" retains the old past participle form; the sense developed after OE times. Cognate
is ModG halten "to hold"; ModE "halt" is borrowed from
French and Italian (those traffic signs, ALT, in Italy
are not just for English-speaking tourists), who borrowed it from German. One holds a holiday, or one
observes it; the sense of "behold" as "look" derives
from this semantic relationship.
Cpds.: be-healdan "BEHOLD, guard"; drēam-healdende
"blissful." (80)

46. wiþ (prep.) "against, opposite, toward, WITH";
wiðer- "against, counter"; [wiðre (n.) "resistance."]

Cognate is ModG wider "against." The prep. is a shortened form of the rare OE adj. wiðer (cf. Gothic wiþra)
which in our texts appears only as a prefix. A "false
friend": the sense "with" is not common; only later in
the MidE period, probably under the influence of the
Scand. cognate viþ, did OE wiþ take on the "accompaniment" sense formerly the function of OE mid.
Cpds.: wiþ-fōn, -grīpan, -habban, -standan; wiðer-lēan,
-ræhtes. (80)

47. be (stressed form bī/biġ) (prep., prefix) "BY,
near, about"; ymb(e) (prep., prefix) "about, around,
near."

Both words are cognate with Lat. ambi-, Gk. amphi-. Be
and bī are related to ModG be- and bei, with the former
unstressed, the latter stressed in each pair. Usually
be as prefix is unstressed before verbs and unemphasized
preps., but stressed (often spelled biġ; -iġ is

virtually the same as -ī) before nouns, or as adverb or
emphasized prep. Ymbe reflects the earlier, longer form
of the same word (as the Lat. and Gk. cognates show).
For the loss of the initial *am- which once preceded
be/bī, compare OE bā (+ þā > BOTH) and Lat. ambō, Gk.
amphō- "both." The ModG um "about" is from the same
root with the latter part missing. The very common prefix be/bī- is not counted in this group.
Cpds.: ymb(e)-beorgan, -clyppan, -fōn, -hweorfan, -ēode,
-sittan, -sittend. (79)

48. findan (a, a, u) (3) "FIND"; -fynde (adj.) "locat-
able"; [ge-fandian (II) "search out, test, experience"];
fundian (II) "strive, direct a course (to), desire (to
go to)"; fēða (wk.m.) "troop on foot, infantry"; [fēðe
(n.) "going, power of locomotion, gait"]; fūs (adj.)
(1) "eager (to go), hastening, ready" (2) "brilliant";
(ge-)fÿsan (I) "impel, prepare."

Probably the original sense of the etymon of the group is
to go or walk. Related would be Gk. patos, pontos "way,
sea"; Lat. pons "bridge"--all with a sense of passage.
(Lat. petere "seek" is a less likely kin.) For the relation between going and the verb find, cf. Lat. invenīre
"to come upon, to find." Fēða is not related to fōt
(Lat. pedem) "foot," but the mnemonic connection is in-
evitable. ModG cognates are finden, Fund "to find,
discovery." Fūs, an admirable word, would now be FOUSE
if it were retained in English; any poet may use it now.
Cpds.: ēaþ-fynde; on-findan; gum-fēða; fēðe-cempa,
-gest, -lāst, -wīg; hin-, ūt-, wæl-fūs; fūs-līc. (78)

49. (ge-)sēon (seah, sāwon, sewen) (5) "SEE, look";
ge-sihþ (f.) "SIGHT, vision"; -sīen "sight"; gesīene (adj.)
"visible."

The IE cognates are unclear: sēon may be related to Lat.
sequi "follow" or to the same root as "say" (Gk. ennepō,
Lat. inquam "I say"), or these may all be related. ModG
cognates are sehen, Sicht, Gesicht "to see, sight,
vision." The ending -þ in ge-sihþ is an IE substantive-
maker, which appears as -(i)t- in Lat. (vanitas, veri-
tas, bonitas), French -ité, ModE -(i)ty, and in several
English words formed from adjectives (health, length,
mirth, truth, etc.). Sēon shows "contraction" of vowels
after an original h sound was lost (*sehan> *seoan> sēon,
with compensatory lengthening). So fōn "take" and hōn
"hang." Sēon also shows Verner's Law in the variation
of the original *h of the infinitive and the w of some
of the pret. forms (cf. weorðan, čēosan).

Cpds.: g̊eond-, ofer-sēon; an-, wǣfer-, wundor-sīen; ēþ-g̊esȳne. (78)

50. eorl (m.) "nobleman, warrior."

The word became the title EARL only late in the OE period, when it took on the Scandinavian sense as the counterpart of the Lat. comes, French comte "count." The Icelandic cognate "jarl" has been revived as an archaizing term among romancers and historians.
Cpds.: eorl-g̊estrēon, -g̊ewǣde, -scipe, -weorod; eorl-līc̊. (77)

51. hild (f.) "battle, warfare."

Like gūþ (No. 39), hild is strictly a poetic word, used as a high-frequency compounder helpful to a poet in search of an initial h (it is not found as the second element of compounds). Both words became obsolete by the twelfth century, as the poetic tradition on which they depended faded. Beowulf accounts for nearly half the occurrences of hild and gūþ in OE. Neither word has certain cognates in Lat. or ModG. Notice that many of the bases compounded with hild are the same ones joined with gūþ: this poetic word-hoard is small and repetitive. Few formulas seem more OE than "hār hilderinc."
Cpds.: hild(e)-bill, -bord, -cumbor, -cyst, -dēor, -freca, -fruma, -g̊eatwe, -g̊ic̊el, -grāp, -hlæmm, -lata, -lēoma, -mēc̊e, -mecg, -rǣs, -rand, -rinc, -sceorp, -setl, -strengo, -swāt, -tūx, -wǣpen, -wīsa. (Hilde-rinc occurs ten times; hilde-dēor eight.) (77)

52. þēod (or þīod) (f.) "people, nation"; þēoden (m.) "prince."

Cf. dryht/dryhten. From the Germanic root of þēod were borrowed the Lat. and Gk. cognates which appear in ModE (from Lat.) as "Teuton." The ModG derivative is Deutsch (< diutisc "people-ish"), the name of the "language of the people," the vulgar (non-Lat.) lang. of Germany. OE þēod (and þēode n.) mean "language" as well, but not in our texts. The only ModE derivative is DUTCH, a word borrowed from Holland before it became specialized on the Continent to refer to the languages and peoples higher up the Rhine.
Cpds.: sig̊e-, wer-þēod; þēod-cyning, -g̊estrēon, -sceaða, -þrēa; el-þēodig̊; þēoden-lēas. (74)

53. <u>fram</u> (prep.) "FROM" (adv.) "forth, away" (adj.)
"froward, brave"; (g̊e-)fremman (I) "further, do, perform, accomplish"; [<u>freme</u> (adj.) "good, kind"; <u>fremu</u> (f.)
"good action, excellence"; <u>fremde</u> (adj.) "foreign,
estranged."]

The evidence for the connection of the prep. and the adj.
is most striking in the Old Norse forms <u>fram</u> "forward"
and <u>fram-r</u> "valiant." The translations "froward" for
<u>fram</u> and "to further" for <u>fremman</u> show the senses de-
veloped from an original spatial sense of the etymon.
The group may be related to the "for" group. Cognate is
ModG <u>fremd</u> "alien," set apart <u>from</u> us. ModE FRO is borrowed from the Scand. cognate of the prep. <u>fram</u>.
Cpds.: sīþ-, un-from; fram-weard; gūþ-fremmend. (73)

54. <u>gold</u> (n.) "GOLD"; <u>gylden</u> (adj.) "GOLDEN"; [g̊eolo
(adj.) "YELLOW."]

Related to <u>gold</u> also is the OE <u>gealla</u> GALL, the yellow
humour. Cognate are Lat. <u>fel</u> "gall," ModG <u>Geld</u>, <u>gelb</u>
"money, yellow." In <u>Beowulf</u>, g̊eolo refers to the color
of linden-wood, the material of shields. The terms for
colors in OE are confusing to us because the OE spectrum
of hues was not divided in quite the same way (e.g.,
their "red" leaned toward the yellow--but see our terms
like "crimson, scarlet, claret, burgundy, velvet, mauve,
lavender, violet, heliotrope, fuchsia, flamingo, peach,
pink, beige"). Even more confusing are the numbers of
OE color terms which denote, not hue (wavelength), but
chroma (reflectivity, brightness, quantity of light) or
intensity (purity, admixture of white or black, lightness
or darkness). ModE also preserves, from OE, the words
"dun, wan, sallow, fallow, bleak, dusky, swarthy, bright,
light, murky, dark, black, gray, white," etc. (as well as
words like "livid, fulvous, sorrel, roan, tawny, pallid,
tan, bay, buff, pale" from Romance langs.) to refer to
"colors" which are not strictly hues. Most speakers
would consider this set of words rather difficult to define, because we are not accustomed to thinking of color
except as hue, in spite of the rather large non-hue resources of our own vocabulary. Adding to the confusion
are OE terms which then referred to chroma (e.g., brūn
and hwīt, meaning "bright, shining," used of BURNished
metal [< brūn]) whose reflexes now (BROWN, WHITE) refer to
hue or intensity. The group of OE, Romance, and ModE
words connected with "black," for instance has not yet
been straightened out (blæc, blāc, blac (?), blīcan,
blæcu, BLACK, BLIK, BLINK, BLAKE, BLEAK, BLEACH, BLOKE,
BLANK, BLANC, etc.): they seem to refer to "black, white,
pale, dark, shiny," like the colorless all-color of Moby
Dick. (On OE colors see <u>MLR</u> 46 and <u>Ang.-Sax. Eng.</u> 3.)
Cpds.: gold-æht, -fāh, -g̊iefa, -hroden, -hwæt, -māðum,

-sele, -weard, -wine, -wlanc; fǣt-gold; eall-gylden;
g̊eolo-rand. (73)

55. lēof (adj.) "dear, beloved"; lufu (f.) "LOVE";
[lufen (f.) "delight, hope"; lufian (II) "LOVE"]; lof
(n.,m.) "praise, renown, glory"; līefan (I) "allow, permit"; g̊e-līefan (I) "beLIEVE."

To hold something dear (lēof) is to believe in it, and
the extension of a LEAVE of absence is a sign of favor
to a dear one. ModG cognates are glauben "to believe"
(Gothic galaubjan), lieb, Liebe "dear, love," Urlaub
Verlaub "furLOUGH, permission," Lob "praise"; kin also is
Lat. lībet "it is permitted," and the Lat. term adopted
by Freud for the erotic principle, libīdo. The adj.
lēof survives in ModE in the phrase "I'd as lief" (I had
just as soon") and "live long day" (= "dear long day"--
lēof simply emphatic) in "I've Been Working on the Rail-
road." From lēof + man came the MidE leman "sweetheart,"
The superl. of lof-g̊eorn, "eager for praise," is the last
word of Beowulf.
Cpds.: lēof-līċ; un-lēof; luf-tācen; eard-, hēah-, mōd-,
sorg-, wīf-lufu; lof-dǣd, -g̊eorn; ā-līefan; lēafnes-word
"permission." (73)

56. ac (conj.) "but."

Those who know Lat. are likely to mistranslate this as
"and" (Lat. ac = atque "and"; Lat. at = "but"). No derivatives survive in ModE. (72)

57. þanc (m. n.) "THANKS"; g̊e-þanc (m.,n.) "thought";
(g̊e-)þancian (II) "THANK"; [æf-þunca (wk.m.) "dismay"];
(g̊e-)þenċan (þōhte) (I) "THINK, consider, intend"; g̊e-
þōht (m.) "THOUGHT"; þynċan (þūhte) (I) "seem, appear."

The sense "thanks" derives from an idea of "favorable
thought," ModG Dank "gratitude." ModG preserves, in
denken "to think" and dünken "seem," the sharp distinc-
tion between the easily confused OE verbs þenċan and
þynċan. The latter appears in ModE only in the archaism
methinks = "it seems to me." The verb þynċan is said to
be the prior one; the notion "to think" develops from a
notion of "to cause to appear (to oneself)," presumably
implying an idea of imagining or fancy, i.e. making images
or phantasms appear before the mind's eye. The verb
þynċan was lost when the similarly pronounced MidE reflex
of þenċan approached too close in meaning, as "it seems
to me" = "I think." Note the i-umlaut relationships which
hold between the vowels of the pres. and pret. tenses

of the two verbs (e/o; y/u); the length of the pret.
vowels compensates for the "lost" n.
Cpds.: fore-, hete-, inwit-, or-, searo-þanc; mōd-ǧeþanc;
þanc-hycgende; ā-, ǧeond-þencan. (72)

58. (ǧe-)faran (ō, ō, a) (6) "go, FARE, proceed"; -fara
(wk.m.) "FARER"; faru (f.) "expedition"; [faroþ (m., n.)
"current, sea"; fær (n.) "vessel"]; fēran (I) "go, FARE";
ǧe-fēran (I) "reach, accomplish"; (ǧe-)ferian (I) "carry,
FERRY"; ǧe-fēra (wk.m.) "companion, retainer"; [fōr (f.)
"voyage"]; ford (m.) "FORD, waterway"; fierd (f.) "army,
military expedition."

Cognate with a group of ModG words like Fahrt "journey,"
fahren "to go, fare," Furt "ford," etc.; with Gk. peirō
"I traverse," poros "way, thoroughFARE"; and with Lat.
portāre "to carry" and porta "door," portus "port," from
the same root with the idea of "passage"; and with FJORD
from the Old Norse. The faran group is probably distantly
related to the advs. for and far (and perhaps even from)
and their numerous relatives, all implying a sense of distance traversed, but the groups are kept distinct in this
list. The p- of the Gk. and Lat. cognates and the f of
the Germanic words are of course classic instances of
Grimm's Law. The fær of this group should not be confused with fær "sudden, FEARful attack." Note how often
the stems of verbs, when an -a is added, appear as wk.m.
agent nouns (cf. -end, -ung): fara, ǧenga, flota, floga,
wealda, etc.
Cpds.: hæǧl-faru; æt-, of-, oþ-ferian; sæ-fōr; fierd-
ǧestealla, -hom, -hræġl, -hwæt, -lēoþ, -rinc, -searo,
-wyrðe. (69)

59. nū (adv.) "NOW" (conj.) "now that."

Cognates Gk. ny, Lat. nunc, ModG nun "now." On the analogy of nū and hū you should be able to translate "How
now, brown cow?" into OE. (69)

60. (ǧe-)sittan (æ, ǣ, e) (5) "SIT"; (ǧe-)settan (I)
"SET, seat, establish"; [ǧe-set (n.) "SEAT"]; setl (n.)
"seat"; [sess (m. [or n.?]) "seat"; sadol (m.) "SADDLE";
sǣta (wk.m.) "one stationed (at a place)."]

ModG cognates are sitzen, setzen, Sitz, "to sit, to set,
seat." The Gk. prefix kata- + the cognate word hedra
"chair" becomes Lat. cathedra "chair, dignitary's or
professor's chair," ecclesiastical Lat. "bishop's seat,"
hence "cathedral"; Lat. cognates of hedra and sittan are
sedēre "to sit," whence many derivatives, and sella

"saddle" (ModG <u>Sattel</u>). In our texts the OE nouns
principally refer to the throne and benches of a mead
hall, as the compounds show. <u>Set</u> is a causal form of
<u>sit</u>, common to the Germanic langs. ModE SETTLE, SETTEE
are derived from this group. ModE SEAT, derives from an
Old Norse form, itself cognate with <u>ge-set</u>.
Cpds.: be-, for-, of-, ofer-, on-, ymb-sittan; ā-, be-
settan; hēah-, hilde-, meodo-setl; flet-, heal-, ymb-
sittend; sadol-beorht; ende-sǣta. (67)

61. <u>micel</u> (adj.) "MUCH, great"; <u>māra</u> (comp.) "MORE,
greater"; <u>mǣst</u> (superl., sb. n.) "greatest, MOST"; <u>mā</u>
(adv. comp., sb. n.) "MORE."

Cognate with Gk. <u>megas</u> "great" (our comb. form MEGALO-),
probably with Lat. <u>magnus</u> "great." The dialect forms
<u>mickle</u> and <u>muckle</u> survive. <u>Mickle</u>, with the <u>i</u> rounded to
<u>y</u> perhaps by analogy with <u>lytel</u>, would yield <u>muckle</u> in
MidE, or <u>muchel</u>, with the <u>k</u> palatalized (as in West
Saxon) in the South, hence by shortening our ModE form
<u>much</u>. <u>Mā</u> also persists in dialect as <u>mo</u>. In MidE, <u>mo</u>
often referred to number and <u>more</u> to size. (66)

62. <u>under</u> (prep., adv.) "UNDER."

Cognate are ModG <u>unter</u>, Lat. <u>infrā</u> "under." (66)

63. (<u>ge-</u>)<u>æðele</u> (adj.) "noble"; <u>æðelu</u> (n.) "noble des-
cent, breeding"; <u>æðeling</u> (m.) "noble, hero, man"; <u>ēðel</u>
(m.) "native land, home."

That these crucial terms died out of the lang. in the
MidE period, presumably under pressure from the French
words reflected in "noble" and "gentle," shows the remarkable influence over the lang. of the Norman aristoc-
racy in England. ModG cognate <u>Adel</u> "nobility." One's
<u>ēðel</u> is the locale of one's <u>æðelu</u>. The word was often
spelled with the rune meaning <u>ēðel</u> in the <u>Beowulf</u> MS.
Perhaps cognate with the IE group of childish names for
"father" which includes Lat. <u>atta</u> "Daddy," and the Gothic
proper name <u>Attila</u> (the Hun).
Cpds.: fæder-æðelu; sib-æðeling; ēðel-riht, -stōl,
-turf, -weard, -wynn. (65)

64. <u>bēag</u> (m.) "ring, crown, necklace"; (<u>ge-</u>)<u>būgan</u> (ēa,
u, o) (2) "BOW (down), sit, retreat"; <u>boga</u> (wk.m.)
"BOW, arch."

The word "bee" from bēag is now obsolete except in nautical use as an iron ring around a spar. The original sense
of būgan is "to turn back," hence the idea of fleeing from
battle (the Maldon sense) as expressed in the cognates Gk.
pheygein, Lat. fugere "to flee." The craven sense of the
verb is common, and affects its use in the Dream of the
Rood. Precious metal bowed into a bēag was the poets'
idea of a noble gift; unlike the verb, the noun has noble
associations.
Cpds.: earm-, heals-bēag "necklace"; bēag-ġiefa, -hroden,
-hord, -sele, -þegu, -wriða; ā-, be-, for·-būgan; wōh-
bogen; flan-, horn-, hring-, stān-boga. (64)

65. (ġe-)licgan (læġ, lāgon, leġen) (5) "LIE (down), lie
dead"; lecgan (leġde) (I) "LAY"; [leġer (n.) "place of
lying, LAIR"; or-leġe (n.) "war, battle"; -legu (wk.f.)
"extent."]

Licgan is cognate with Gk. lechos, Lat. lectus "bed," and
ModG liegen, legen, Lager "to lie, to lay, bed (or beer
for laying away)," etc. LAW (< OE lagu) derives from the
group, but was borrowed in late OE times from Old Norse,
meaning "that which is set down" (cf. OE dōm, Gk. themis
[No. 26], Lat. statutum, ModG Gesetz). In or-lege and
feorh-legu the sense of "what is established" (the fate
of war; the fixed extent of life) which lies behind "law"
can be seen. (Lat. lēx is thought to be related not to
this group, but to Lat. legere "to gather, read.")
Cpds.: ā-licgan; ā-lecgan; leġer-bed; or-leġ-hwīl;
feorh-legu. (64)

66. lang (adj.) "LONG"; lenġra (comp.) "LONGER";
ġe-lang/ġe-lenġe (adj.) "at hand, ALONG with, beLONGing
to"; lange (adv.) "long, for a long time"; leng (comp.
adv.) "longer"; lenġest (superl. adv.) "longest, for the
longest time"; [langoþ (m.) "longing"]; langung (f.)
"LONGING, anxiety."

The connection of "along" and "belong" with "long" seems
to arise from the idea of LENGTH of equal dimension as
suggesting the idea of parallel accompaniment, and from
the idea of extension in an opposing direction (and-long)
as extension lengthwise, parallelism, accompaniment.
LONGING is anxiety caused by one's long distance (in
space or time) from an object of desire. Cognate are
ModG lang, langen "long, to reach" and Lat. longus "long."
Cpds.: and-, ealdor-, morgen-, niht-, up-lang; lang-
ġestrēon, -sum, -twīdiġ; langung-hwīl. (63)

67. heard (adj.) "HARD, fierce, bitter, strong";
hearde (adv.) "HARD, sorely."

Cognate are ModG hart "hard" and Gk. kartos "strength."
The three senses of "materially tough," "difficult," and
"unyielding" are all already joined in OE and before.
For the ModE a for OE (LWS) ea, see eall (No. 7).
Cpds.: fēol-, for-, fȳr-, īren-, nīþ-, reġn-, scūr-,
wīġ-heard; heard-ecg, -hycgende, -līce. (62)

68. māðum/māððum (m.) "treasure, precious object, ornament"; ġe-mǣne (adj.) "common, in common"; [ġe-māna
(wk.m.) "fellowship, meeting"]; mān (n.) "crime, wicked-
ness."

Over two-thirds of the occurrences of māðum in OE poetry
are in Beowulf. Cognates are ModG gemein "common"; Lat.
mūnus, mūtāre, mutuus, communis "gift, to change, mutual,
common." The root sense, if the relation of the words of
this group is correct, is "change"; exchange of gifts
(māðum); reciprocation of friendship (ġe-mǣne); change
for the worse (mān). As the Last Survivor in Beowulf
knew, māðum is mutable. ModE MEAN derives from ġe-mǣne,
and became a synonym of "inferior" in the same way "common" (< communis) and "vulgar" (< Lat. vulgus "the
people") took on pejorative senses. The ġe- of ġe-mǣne
is the "copulative prefix" seen in ġe-sibbe, ġe-stealla,
ġe-selda, ġe-sīþ, ġe-lenġe, etc., meaning "accompanying,"
and often implying fellowship (cf. Lat. cum of comrade,
companion, French compère, etc.).
Cpds.: māðum-ǣht, -fæt, -ġestrēon, -ġiefa, -ġifu, -siġle,
-sweord, -wela; dryht-, gold-, hord-, ofer-, sinc-, wun-
dur-māðum; mān-for-dǣdla, -scaða. (62)

69. (ġe-)wealdan (ēo, ēo, ea) (7) "have power over,
WIELD, rule"; wealdend (m.) "ruler," esp. "the Lord";
ġe-weald (n.) "control"; [wealda (wk.m., adj.) "omnipo-
tent, God."]

Presumably from an IE root "to be strong," hence Lat.
valēre and many ModE derivatives from the Lat. and
Romance langs.: valor, value, valence, avail, etc.
Cpds.: al-, an-walda; on-weald. (62)

70. hand (f.) "HAND"; ġe-hende (prep.) "near, at hand."

ModG cognate Hand. The prep. is "post-positive" like
many in OE which follow their object: the fine line is
"hē læġ þeġn-līce þēodne ġehende" "he lay down and died
as a thane should, next to his lord" (Maldon, l. 294).

Þegn and þēoden are knit in alliteration, and in death.
The ModE HANDY is cognate, but not a direct descendent of
ge-hende. Hand is often spelled hond (cf. mann/monn;
nama/noma; dranc/dronc; fram/from; and/ond, etc.) indicating that at one time a following nasal consonant
affected the quality of short back vowels.
Cpds.: hand-bona, -gemōt, -gesella, -gestealla, -geweorc,
-gewriðen, -locen, -plega, -rǣs, -scolu, -sporu, -wundor;
īdel-hende "empty-handed." (61)

71. hyge (m.) "mind, thought, heart, courage"; ge-hygd
(f.,n.) "thought"; hygdig (adj.) "mindful" (suffix)
"-minded"; (ge-)hycgan (hogode) (III) (and II) "think,
intend, resolve"; [for-hycgan "despise"]; hyht (m.) "expectation of joy, hope."

Hyge and hyht are not etym. connected with the ModE
"hope." Neither important word nor their derivatives are
recorded after the 13th c.; ModG has also lost the group.
In these cases it seems likely that the requirement in
alliterative poetry for a multitude of synonyms with different initials for common concepts sustained words in
the language which became obsolete as the alliterative
tradition faded.
Cpds.: hyge-mǣðu, -rōf, -þīhtig, -þrym, -bend, -giōmor,
-mēðe, -sorh; ofer-, won-hygd; ofer-hycgan; bealo-,
heard-, swīþ-, stīþ-, þanc-, wīs-hycgende; an-, bealo-,
grom-, nīþ-, þrist-hygdig; brēost-, mōd-gehygd. (61)

72. ge-munan (-man, -manst, -munde) (pret.-pres.) "be
MINDful of, remember"; myne (m.) "thought, favor"; mynd
(f.) "thought"; myntan (I) "intend, think"; ge-mynd (f.)
"memory, remembrance"; (ge-)myndgian (II) "reMIND";
(ge-)manian (II) "exhort, admonish."

Cognate with Lat. mens, memini, monēre, mentīre "mind, I
remember, to advise, to lie"; Gk. mnēstis, memona "memory,
yearn," with such interesting relatives as Minerva, money,
Eumenides, mania, automatic, maenad, -mancy, monster.
Oddly, the ModE word "mean" (from OE mǣnan "mean, tell,
lament") cannot certainly be connected with this group.
The words in Lat., Gk., and OE meaning "be mindful" are
all pret.-pres. (memini, memona, munan). The OE poets
treat the words of this group as if the ideas of memory
and intention which they imply were of special importance.
In these last two articles and elsewhere in the list,
notice that groups of related words tend to maintain the
quantity of the stem vowel: all these words have short
vowels. The "lengthened" ablaut grade, visible in strong
verbs, and other factors, will disturb their symmetry.
Cpds.: on-munan; ge-myndig; weorþ-mynd "honor." (61)

73. word (n.) "WORD, speech."

Cognate are ModG Wort, Lat. verbum "word," and Gk. eirein "to speak," hence rhētōr "speaker" (> RHETORIC). Cpds.: bēot-, g̊ylp-, lāst-, lēafnes-, meðel-, þrȳþ-word; word-cwide "speech," -g̊yd, -hord, -riht. (60)

74. dæg̊ (pl. dagas) (m.) "DAY"; dōgor (n.) "day."

An OE verb from the same root, dagian, gives us dawn (MidE daw). OE g, g̊, often appear as w, y in MidE and ModE (cf. būgan "bow," mæg̊ "may"). The group is not cognate with Lat. dies "day." The daisy is the day's eye, like the sun (dæg̊es ēage). The ā in the plural forms of dæg̊ is from an earlier æ, lowered because of the back vowel (a or u) in the following syllable (cf. hwæl stæf "staff/staves," pæþ, fæt "vessel"). Cpds.: ǣr-, dēaþ-, dōm-, ealdor-, ende-, hearm-, lǣn-, līf-, swylt-, tīd-, win-dæg̊; dæg̊-hwīl, -rīm, -weorc; ende-dogor; fyrn-, g̊ēar-dagas "days of yore." (59)

75. (g̊e-)weorc (n.) "WORK, pain"; (g̊e-)wyrċan (worhte) (I) "make, WORK, achieve"; [g̊e-wyrht (f.) "deed."]

Cognates: ModG Werk "work" and wirken "to effect, feel pain"; Gk. ergon "activity," whence energy, organ, liturgy, George, orgy, surgeon. ModE WROUGHT < worhte (the pret.); the ModE suffix -WRIGHT (playwright, wheelwright, etc.) is from the same etymon. The association of the term "work" with the idea of distress (cf. labor, toil, travail) is ancient; we feel medicine "work" in a wound. Cpds.: beadu-, dæg̊-, ellen- "valorous deed," heaðo-, niht-weorc; hand-, land-, nīþ-g̊eweorc; be-wyrċan; eald-g̊ewyrht. (59)

76. guma (wk.m.) "man."

Found in poetry only; cognate with Lat. homo, nēmo "man, no-one" and perhaps with humus "soil," Gk. chthonos "under-worldly." ModE "bridegroom" replaced, in the sixteenth century, the earlier "brideGOME." "Groom" itself (= "boy") is of uncertain origin. The word gome retains its native and poetic flavor in MidE verse. Cpds.: dryht-, seld-guma; gum-cynn, -cyst, -drēa, -dryhten, -fēða, -mann. (58)

77. sele (m.) "hall"; sæl (n.) "hall"; [sæld/seld (n.)
"hall"]; ge-selda (wk.m.) "cohabitor, companion."

Cognate are ModG Saal, French salle (whence SALON, SALOON),
and Italian sala (the French and Italian borrowed from the
Germanic) "hall, room." The OE words are rarely found in
prose.
Cpds.: sele-drēam, -drēorig, -ful, -gyst, -rædend, -rest,
-secg, -þegn, -weard; bēah-, bēor-, dryht-, eorþ-, gest-,
gold-, gūþ-, hēah-, hring-, hrōf-, nīþ-, wīn-sele; seld-
guma; medu-, cear-seld. (58)

78. sweord (n.) "SWORD."

Cognate with ModG Schwert.
Cpds.: sweord-bealo, -freca, -gifu; eald-, gūþ-, māððum-,
wæg-sweord. (58)

79. hātan (hēt/heht, hēton, hāten) (7) "name, call, command"; ge-hātan (7) "promise, threaten"; [ōretta (wk.m.)
"warrior"; ōnettan (I) "hasten."]

The verb hātan is doubly interesting grammatically. It
is the only example in English of the "middle" or "syn-
thetic" passive-voiced verb, in its sense "be called":
"he HIGHT" means "he is named" (this use does not occur in
our texts). The only OE forms are hātte, hātton, "he
(they) is or was called." It is also one of the few verbs
(cf. lācan/leolc; ondrædan/ondreord; lætan/leort; rædan/
reord) which still show the signs of "reduplication" in
their preterites (typical of class 7), alongside normalized pret. forms (hēt, lēc, ondrēd, lēt, rēd). Like many
IE verbs, these prets. were formed with a doubling of the
stem (cf. Lat. do/dedi). The words ōret- and ōnettan are
related to hātan by an idea of "calling against" as "to
challenge" (Gothic and-haitjan), esp. a challenge to combat or to a race. The pre-historic forms of the words,
*or-hāt and on-hātjan, show the presence of hātan. Cog-
nate with Lat. ciēre, ModG heissen "to call."
Cpd.: ōret-mecg "warrior." (57)

80. fæst (adj.) "firm, fixed"; fæste (adv.) "firmly,
FAST"; (ge-)fæstnian (II) "FASTEN, confirm"; [fæstnung (f.)
"firmness"]; fæsten (n.) "FASTNESS, retreat, place of
safety."

The word fæst is used exclusively in the sense "to stick
FAST" in OE. The later development of the word, first as
an adverb, to mean "speedily," is explained when one looks
at the ModG fast "almost, close upon": a fast runner is

one who sticks close to his swifter rivals. Other ModG
cognates are fest, befestigen "firm, to fasten."
Cpds.: ār-, blǣd-, ġin-, sigor-, sōþ-, stede-, tīr-,
þrymm-, wīs-fæst; fæst-līče,-rǣd. (56)

81. mǣre (adj.) "illustrious, famous"; mǣrðu (f.) "fame,
glory, glorious deed."

The ModG Mär "news, report" and Märchen "fairy tale,
legend" are related to these words by a sense of renown;
like ġe-friġnan, they hark back to an oral culture. Perhaps also mā and its relatives are cognate. Abstract
nouns in-ð are often feminine (cf. Lat. -itas).
Cpds.: fore-, heaðo-mǣre; ellen-mǣrðu. (55)

82. weard (m.) "guardian, lord"; weard (f.) "watch, protection"; -wearde "guarded"; weardian (II) "guard, occupy,
remain behind"; warian (II) "guard, keep, inhabit"; -ware
(m.pl.), -wara (f.pl.) "dwellers, people."

Cognate with ModG Wart, wahren "keeper, to watch over,"
Gk. ōra "care," Lat. verēri "to revere, fear." Perhaps
OE wǣre "pledge, protection," wearn "hindrance, refusal,"
and warnian "warn" are also related. French borrowed
from Germanic its word guard (cf. William/Guillaume; war/
guerre; wily/guile [?] for Germanic w-/French gu- pairs).
WARD took on its sense of "kept" (as a foster-child, like
Batman's ally Robin) rather than "keeper" by the 15th c.
The OE word hlāford (> Scottish "laird," ModE "lord") and
its compounds occur sixteen times in our texts. It derives from hlāf "bread" (> LOAF) + weard; the lord is the
guardian of the bread (as the lady, hlǣfdiġe, is in charge
of making the bread). Hlāford is not counted here.
Cpds.: bāt-, brycg-, eorþ-, ēðel-, gold-, hord-, hȳþ-,
land-, ren-, sele-, yrfe-weard; ǣġ-, eoton-, ferh-, hēafod-
weard (f.); or-wearde; bealu-, burg-ware; land-waru. (55)

83. eorðe (wk.f.) "EARTH."

Cognate with ModG Erde, perhaps Gk. era "earth." In poetry
esp., it competed with middan-ġeard in the sense of "world."
Cpds.: eorþ-cyning, -draca, -hūs, -reċed, -scræf, -sele,
-weall, -weard, -weġ, -wela. (53)

84. folc (n.) "people, army, FOLK."

32

ModG cognate <u>Volk</u>. The original sense may have been the
military one. <u>Flock</u>--OE <u>flocc</u>--is obscure in origin, but
may derive from this word by an unusual (for OE) metathesis (inversion of letters). Perhaps related to <u>fela</u>
(No. 28).
Cpds.: folc-āgende, -cwēn, -cyning, -rēd, -riht, -scaru,
-stede, -toga; biġ-, siġe-folc. (53)

85. hwīl (f.) "space of time, WHILE"; <u>hwīlum</u> (dat. pl.
of <u>hwīl</u>) "sometimes, formerly, WHILOM."

"Whilom" had the sense "once upon a time" for centuries.
Cognate with ModG <u>Weile</u> "while"; Lat. <u>quiēs</u>, <u>tranquillus</u>
"rest, quiet."
Cpds.: dæġ-, earfoþ-, ġescæp-, langung-, orleġ-, siġe-
hwīl. (53)

86. <u>wæl</u> (n.) "the slain, slaughter, field of battle."

The OE word is now known esp. from Wagner's <u>Walküre</u>, the
Old Norse <u>Valkyrja</u> (ModE Valkyrie) "chooser of the slain,"
one of the twelve war-demons who bore corpses from the
battlefield to the Scandinavian military heaven, VALhalla,
the "hall of the slain." Like <u>gūþ</u> and <u>hild</u>, <u>wæl</u> is a use-
ful compounder.
Cpds.: wæl-bedd, -bend, -blēat, -dēaþ, -drēor, -fǣhþ,
-fāg, -feall, -feld, -fūs, -fyll, -fyllo, -fȳr, -gǣst,
-ġīfre, -hlemm, -nīþ, -rǣs, -rēaf, -rēc, -rēow, -rest,
-sceaft, -seax, -sleaht, -spere, -steng, -<u>stōw</u> "place of
slaughter," -wulf. (53)

87. <u>wrecan</u> (æ, ǣ, e) (5) "drive (out), banish, avenge,
utter, recite"; <u>ġe-wrecan</u> (5) "avenge, punish"; [<u>wracu</u>
(f.) "revenge, misery"]; <u>wræc</u> (n.) "persecution, misery,
exile"; <u>wrecċa</u> (wk.m.) "an exile, adventurer"; [<u>wrecend</u>
(m.) "revenger."]

The Lat. cognate <u>urgēre</u> "to URGE, push, drive" suggests
the original sense of the root of this group. The ModG
cognate <u>rächen</u> "to avenge" corresponds to the OE development of the sense, but another ModG cognate, <u>Recke</u> "hero,
warrior," shows a line of development of meaning abandoned
by English in favor of the notion of exile and torment.
The heroic and tormented senses are nearly joined, however,
in the word <u>wrecċa</u>, whose ModE reflex is WRETCH: Klaeber
glosses the word "exile, adventurer, hero"--a man on his
own was potentially a hero. But as the elegies show, the
life of exile was felt to be mainly wretched: few words

in the elegies are as stern as wræc-lāstas "paths of
exile." We can still use WREAK (< wrecan) not only of
vengeance but of an utterance: one "drives forth" or
vents his feelings in speech, esp. by making a poem. At
this point the verb is easily confused with reċċan in one
of its senses, "to narrate." MidE evidence suggests that
a word wrǣc (f.) may have been in variation with wrǣc
(n.), but the OE metrical evidence is insufficient to
determine the length of the vowel. ModE WRECK comes from
early French, ultimately derived from the same stem as
WRACK (< wræc).
Cpds.: ā-, for-wrecan; un-wrecen; ġyrn-, nȳd-wracu;
wræc-lāst, -mæcg, -sīþ. (53)

88. wītan (ā, i, i) (1) "impute, blame"; wīte (n.) pun-
ishment, torment"; [wĭtnian (II) "punish. torment";
ed-wīt- (n.) "reproach, disgrace"]; ġe-wītan (1) "go,
depart, betake, die"; wuton/uton (hortatory auxiliary)
"let us."

From the idea of "seeing" which lies behind the related
group witan "know" (No. 29) comes the idea of WITnessing
and hence charging with blame, wītan. Compare the Lat.
animadvertere "to turn one's attention to, to observe, to
blame." From blaming to punishing was a step taken in
several Germanic langs. The very frequent verb ġe-wītan
"go" (always with ġe- in our texts) likewise derives its
meaning from "to see": one looks at a place intending to
go there, and then (perfective ġe-) one goes. The word
ġe-wītan is often accompanied by a verb of motion in the
infinitive, and a reflexive pronoun (Him Scyld ġewāt . . .
feran "Scyld went (betook himself off) carrying"--Beowulf
26-7). From the base of ġe-wītan, the 1st person pl.
subjunctive "let us go" is wuton, often shortened
(uniquely) to uton. Its use as "let's" in general, with
an infinitive, may be compared with the French allons.
Wītan, wĭtan, and ġe-wītan are easily confused; remember
that witan is a pret.-pres. verb. ModE TWIT is from æt-
wĭtan "reproach" by "false division" (the t taken from
the prefix and affixed to the base).
Cpds.: æt-, oþ-wītan; ed-wīt-līf, forþ-ġewītan. (52)

89. hord (n.) "HOARD, treasure."

The common compound hord-weard usually refers to the
dragon in Beowulf. Cognate is ModG Hort "hoard." The
root may indicate something hidden.
Cpds.: hord-ærn, -burh, -cofa, -ġestrēon, -māðum, -weard,
-wela, -weorðung, -wynn, -wyrðe; bēah-, brēost-, word-,
wyrm-hord. (51)

90. manig (adj., pron.) "MANY a" (pl.) "many"; menigu
(f.) "multitude."

Like the ModG cognate manch, manig can modify a singular
noun, where we must translate "many a." Kin to menigu is
ModG Menge "quantity, crowd."
Cpd.: for-manig. (51)

91. sum (adj., pron.) "one, a certain (one), SOME, someone, a special one"; sin- "continual, great"; [sim(b)le
(adv.) "always."]

In the U.S. version of ModE the phrase "some men" is am-
biguous unless we mark stress: "some mén" means "a few
men, certain men"; "sóme mèn" means "unusually interesting
men, very good men" ("thóse were sóme tomàtoes"). This
latter, emphatic sense is not a direct derivative of OE
usage, but it is frequent in OE, especially when sum is
accompanied by a partitive genitive:
                              Næfre ic māran geseah
     eorla ofer eorþan,   ðonne is ēower sum,
     secg on searwum;   nis þæt seldguma . . . .
                              (Beowulf 247-9)
"I never saw a greater noble on earth than that one among
you, that warrior in his armor; that's no courtly fop . .
. ." The OE idiom twelfa sum usually means "one in a
company of twelve, including the one," although sometimes
it means "one of thirteen." If everything is one, conceived temporally it is perpetual, and conceived spatially
it is of vast extent: so sum in its etym. sense of "one"
is related to sin-. The cognates make the relationship
clear: Gk. heis "one," Lat. semper, simplex, semel, simul
"always, simple, once, like." Apparently the only ModE
reflex of sin- is the name of an evergreen plant, "sen-
green" (a leek or a periwinkle), ModG Sinngrün. Sin- is
easy to confuse with synn "wrong," sometimes used as a
prefix and spelled like sin-. "Some" is spelled with o
for the original u for the same reason as are "come"
(No.32) and "worm" (No. 184), which see. Related to this
group also is the suffix -some (ModE lonesome, OE longsum
"long-lasting," ModG langsam "slow"), but the suffix is
not counted here.
Cpds.: sin-dolh, -frēa, -gāl, -gāla, -gāles, -here,
-niht, -snæd. (51)

92. (ge-)scieppan (scōp, scōpon, scapen) (6) "create,
SHAPE, allot"; scieppend (m.) "(the) Creator"; (ge)-sceaft
(f.) "creation, destiny, allotment"; sceaft(ig) (adj.)
"possessed of, allotted"; [ge-sceap/ge-scipe (n.) "creation, destiny, the SHAPE of things"]; -scipe (m.) "-SHIP,
state of."

The compounds of sceaft esp. preserve the primitive fatalistic and passive sense of the group, that which has been
shaped for one, one's fate (cf. wyrd No. 23, giefeðe No.
43). As often (Dēmend, Hǣlend, Wealdend) the group pro-
vides an active and Christian term, Scieppend, the providential and creative God, the Shaper. A word which looks
as if it is related to this group, scop "poet, singer,"
is not related. Those who translate or refer to scop as
"the Shaper" indulge in false etymology, on the analogy of
Gk. poiēsis "making, poetry." (The relations of scop are
with ModE "scoff" and its ancestors: in the primitive
sense he was a satirist--in Icelandic saga, scurrilous
derogatory verses often became elements of feuds. Cf.
Lat. mimus.) Cognate with the scieppan are ModG Schöpfung,
Geschöpf, schaffen "creation, creature, to create."
Sceaft "spear-shaft" is probably related to this group, but
is not counted here.
Cpds.: earm-sceapen; forþ-, līf-, mǣl-gesceaft; fēa-
"possessed of little, destitute," frum-, ġeō-, meotod-,
won-sceaft; ġeō-sceaft-gāst; fēa-sceaftiġ; hēah-ġesceap;
ġe-scæp-hwīl; dryht-, eorl- "nobility, noble deeds,"
fēond-, frēond-, lēod-scipe. (50)

93. sǣ (m. or f.) "SEA."

The relations of this word are uncertain: perhaps kin to
Gk. haima "blood," or to the root of OE sīgan "to sink."
Note that it is always the first element in its many compounds (there are twenty-one separate words) in our texts.
In Beowulf, the hero is challenged about his prowess in
swimming. His challenger Unferþ displays his own prowess
with watery words, as he varies the term sǣ with a choice
thesaurus of synonyms (ll. 506-519): sǣ, sund, wǣd, wæter,
ēagorstrēam, merestrǣta, gārsecg, ġeofon, ȳþ, wylm, holm.
This by no means exhausts the hoard of words the insular
nation kept for the sea (brim, lagu, hron-rād, etc.). At
the end of the series, Unferþ adds a set of terms which,
by evoking the pleasures of the return to land, suggests
the sort of northerners' attitude to the sea felt in The
Seafarer:
    ðonon hē gesōhte   swǣsne ēþel
    lēof his lēodum,   lond Brondinga,
    freoðoburh fægere,   þǣr hē folc āhte,
    burh ond bēagas.
"From there he sought out his own dear country, the nation
to whom he was dear, the land of the Brondings, that fair
town of peace, where he had people, and town, and rings."
Cpds.: sǣ-bāt, -cyning, -dēor, -draca, -fōr, -ġēap, -gen-
ga, -grund, -lāc, -lād, -lida, -līðend, -mann, -mēðe,
-næss, -rinc, -sīþ, -weall, -wong, -wudu, -wylm. (49)

36

94. weg̊ (m.) "WAY, route, road"; wegan (æ, ǣ, e) (5)
"carry, wear, have (feelings)"; wǣg̊ (m.) "wave, surf";
[wǣn/wǣg̊n (m.) "WAGON, WAIN"]; wicg̊ (n.) "steed."

The group is cognate with the Lat. vehere "to carry" (but
probably not to the Lat. via "way"); also to Gk. ochos
"wagon"; ModG Weg, bewegen, wägen, wiegen, Woge "way,
to move, to weigh (transitive), to weigh (intransitive),
wave." ModE WEIGH comes from the sense of lifting as if
to carry; WAG from the sense of moving (the ModE noun and
verb "wave" are not related, but identical in sense to
words from this group). Wǣg̊ "wave" must come from a sense
of a current bearing across a stretch of water in billows.
Wicg̊ is a poetic word, rare in prose. ModE AWAY is from
the phrase "on weg̊" taken as a single word.
Cpds.: æt-, for-wegan; eorþ-, feor-, flōd, fold-, forþ-
hwæl-, on-weg̊; wīd-wegas; wǣg̊-bora, -flota, -holm,
-līðend, -sweord. (49)

95. þeg̊n (m.) "THANE, retainer, minister, servant";
[þēnian (II) "serve."]

Macbeth has kept the word familiar. The original sense
was "child, boy"; cf. the Gk. cognate teknon "child,"
from an IE root meaning "to beget." ModG cognate Degen
"thane." The verb shows lengthening of the vowel in compensation for loss of the g̊.
Cpds.: būr-, ealdor-, heal-, mago- "young retainer,"
ombiht-, sele-þeg̊n; þeg̊n-līce, -sorg. (48)

96. oft (adv.) "OFTen" (comp.) oftor (superl.) oftost.

Very likely cognate with ofer group, but kept separate in
this list. Cognate with ModG oft. ModE often is an
extended form, which came into use in MidE for obscure
reasons. (47)

97. ōðer (adj., sb.) "OTHER, the other, one of two,
second, another."

The word ōðer is always declined strong. It is the normal
ordinal numeral in OE for the ModE "second." (The ordi-
nals for 1-5 are forma/fyrest/ǣrest, ōðer, þridda, fēorða,
fīfta.) Cognate with ōðer are ModG ander "other" (cf.
Gothic anþar, Skt. ántara), Gk. enioi "some," Lat. enim
"for," and probably with Lat. alius, alter "other" (and
hence with OE elles "ELSE" and its relatives, but the
groups are kept separate in this list). (47)

98. (ğĕ-)secgan (sæğde) (III) "SAY, tell"; [ğe-seğen (f.) "SAYING, tale."]

The OE sagu (cf. Old Norse SAGA), from which the ModE word SAW "old saying" derives, does not occur in our texts. Secgan may be cognate with Gk. ennepe (< *in-seque) "say (imperative)," Lat. inquam (< *in-squam) "I say." Pret. forms of secgan often omit the ğ and show compensatory lengthening (sæde).
Cpds.: ā-secgan; eald-ğeseğen. (47)

99. wer (m.) "man, male"; weorold (f.) "WORLD."

In The Faerie Queene, Spenser indulges in an etymology of "world," deriving it from war old "of ancient strife." He is not far wrong; weorold is from the roots of wer + eald "old" (in its sense of "time, life"), more visibly in the Old High German weralt (> ModG Welt "world"). Cf. Lat. saeculum, which means "the age of man," and developed the senses of "world" (as in secular, "worldly, mundane") and "time" (as in the French siècle, "century"). Eald is treated and counted elsewhere (No. 13). Wer is cognate with Lat. vir "man, hero," the base of the word "virtue": notice that because r and w are not affected by the sound changes described in Grimm's Law, the words wer and vir still closely resemble one another. OE wer is preserved in WEREwolf "wolf-man."
Cpds.: wer-þēod; weorold-ār, -candel, -cyning, -ende, -ğesǣliğ, -rīče. (47)

100. bīdan (ā, i, i) (1) "BIDE, remain, wait, dwell"; ğe-bīdan (1) "live to experience, await, undergo"; [bid (n.) "aBIDing, halt."]

The verbs are easily confused with biddan "ask" and bædan "compel" (No. 218): the "length" of the vowels of ModE "bide/bid" helps keep bīdan/biddan separate. The ğe- prefixed verb shows sharply perfective sense, the accomplishment of the action initiated by waiting, waiting through to the end, and hence having experienced or endured (often with a connotation of suffering hardship--"I can't abide this weather!").
Cpds.: ā-, on-bīdan. (46)

101. ğearu (adj.) "ready, prepared, equipped"; ğeare/ğearwe (adv.) "readily, surely"; -ğearwe (f.) "GEAR"; (ğe-)ğierwan (I) "prepare, equip, adorn."

Cognate is the ModG adv. gar "completely, quite." The ModE
YARE "ready" is virtually obsolete except for nautical use
("shipshape"); nautical terminology is extremely conserva-
tive of old forms (cf. bee < bēag; wale < walu; yard < ġeard;
belay < belecgan; gangway < gang + weġ, etc.--words otherwise lost from the language).
Cpds.: ġearu-līċe; eall-ġearo; on-ġierwan; fæðer-ġearwe
"feather-gear, plumage." (46)

102. *mōtan (mōt, mōst, mōste) (pret.-pres.) "may, be permitted, MUST."

Cognate is ModG müssen "must," and perhaps OE metan "measure" (but the words are kept separate in this list). The
ModE reflex must is from the OE pret. subjunctive form; it
is a "false friend"--the sense "may" is much more common,
and closer to the original Germanic sense of the stem,
of "having enough room." (46)

103. god (m.) "GOD" (n.) "god."

The word is not related to OE gōd "good"; cf. OE man
"one," mān "crime." Such pairs show the phonemic force of
vowel length in OE. The pre-history of this Germanic word
(ModG Gott) is obscure. (45)

104. oþ/oþ-þæt/oþ-þe (prep., conj.) "until"; oþ- "away,
off."

The disjunctive prefix is not counted here. The conjunction oþþe should not be confused with its homophone oþþe
"or." (45)

105. frēogan (II) "love, favor"; frēond (m.) "FRIEND";
[frēod (f.) "friendship, peace"]; friþ (m.) frioðu (wk.f.)
"peace, safety, refuge"; [frēo (f.) "lady"]; frēo- (adj.)
"FREE, noble, dear."

The Skt. word prī "to endear" lies near the root of this
group. The step from frēod to friþ is easy enough seman-
tically. Those most dear, in a household, are the relatives of the head, not the slaves: hence the dear are
the free. Compare the Lat. līberī "children," literally
"the free ones" in the household. Frederick (Friedrich)
means "peaceful ruler." Friday is the day of Frigg, a
Scand. goddess who was the beloved lady of Odin (for whom

Wednesday was named). The pl. of freond is normally
friend, but the -as pl. sometimes occurs.
Cpds.: freond-lar, -laðu, -leas, -lice, -scipe; frioðo-
burh, -sibb, -wær, -webbe, -wong; fen-freoðo; freo-burh,
-dryhten, -lic, -mæg, -wine. (44)

106. (ge-)niman (a, a, u) (4) "take, seize, take off,
kill."

Cognate with ModG nehmen "to take"; prob. Gk. nemein,
nomos "to distribute, law"; Lat. numerus "number." The
ppl. "taken (with cold)" is ModE NUMB; also derived from
the etymon is NIMBLE, which first meant quick to take in
learning, clever, nimble-witted. Niman was driven out by
"take," borrowed from Scand.
Cpds.: be-, for-niman "take away, destroy." (44)

107. sunu (m.) "SON."

ModG Sohn, Gk. hyios "son" are cognate. The word is a
"u-stem" noun with unusual case endings in -a in gen.,
dat.sg., and nom. pl. In poetry the word often begins a
formula, followed by a proper name in the genitive. (44)

108. ellen (n.) "courage, valor, strength, zeal."

Another heroic term prominent in Beowulf and lost from
English.
Cpds.: mægen-ellen; ellen-dæd, -gæst, -lice, -mærðu,
-rof, -sioc, -weorc "deeds of valor." (43)

109. self (pron.) "SELF."

Cognate is ModG selb; perhaps the initial s is related
to the German and Lat. reflexive pronouns sich and se.
The word often has more intensive than reflexive force
in OE. (43)

110. *þurfan (þearf, þearft, þorfte) (pret.-pres.)
"need, have reason"; þearf (f.) "need, distress";
[þearfa (wk.m.) "one in need"; ge-þearfian (II)
"necessitate."]

Cognate with ModG bedürfen, Bedarf "to need, requirement."
Cpds.: fyren-, nearo-þearf. (43)

111. ecg (f.) "EDGE, sword."

A favorite metonymy of the poets. Ecg is cognate with
ModG Eck(e) "angle, edge"; Gk. akmē "acme" (with a sense
"pimple," hence acne); Lat. aciēs "edge, point" and with
EAR or spike of wheat.
Cpds.: ecg-bana, -clif, -hete, -þracu; brūn-, heard-
stȳl-ecg. (42)

112. hæleþ/hæle (m.) "man, warrior, hero."

Cognate with ModG Held "hero" as in Heldentenor, in
Wagner. Like æðele, a noble word lost from the language.
(42)

113. dugan (dēag, dohte) (pret.-pres.) "avail, be good
for, be strong"; duguþ (f.) (1) "company of tried retainers, host" (2) "power, excellence, virtue"; ge-
dīgan (I) "survive, endure"; dyhtig (adj.) "DOUGHTY,
strong, good."

Cognate with ModG taugen, Tugend "to be good for, virtue"; Gk. tychē "fortune." If DOUTH had survived into
ModE (< duguþ) it might have been used, as it was in OE,
in contrast to geoguþ (> YOUTH) "the inexperienced among
the band of retainers" (No. 119), as a more forceful term
for the virtues of maturity than "middle-aged." (41)

114. feor(r) (adv.) "FAR, long ago"; feorran (adv.)
"from aFAR"; [feorran (I) "take away."]

Cognate with ModG fern, entfernt "far, remote"; Gk.
perā "further." The group is probably related to fyrn
"former," and ultimately to for (No. 11), but the words
are kept apart in this list.
Cpds.: feor-būend, -cȳþþ, -weg; feorran-cund. (41)

115. lāst (m.) "track, footprint"; lǣstan (I) "follow,
serve"; ge-lǣstan (I) "serve, fulfill"; lār (f.) "in-
struction, counsel, LORE"; (ge-)lǣran (I) "teach";

[leornian (II) "LEARN"; list (m., f.) "skill."]

The cobbler's LAST is a sort of wooden footprint. Cognate are ModG Leisten, Geleise "shoemaker's last, track";
Lat. līra "furrow." (Someone who is delirious has gone
off the track.) If you have followed the track of a subject, you have learned it; hence the connection of lāst
and lār. Cognate are ModG Lehre, lernen, List "doctrine,
to learn, cunning." In OE leornian and lǣran have their
modern senses only; in MidE they confusingly retained
their old senses, but learn came also to mean "teach"
and lere also to mean "learn." Now to "learn" someone
about a subject is considered bad usage, in spite of its
antiquity.
Cpds.: lāst-word; feorh-, fēðe-, fōt-, wræc-lāst; ful-
lǣstan/fylstan "help"; lār-cwide; frēond-lār. (41)

116. wīd (adj.) "WIDE, extended"; wīde (adv.) "widely,
far."

Cognate with ModG weit "wide." Both feorr and wīd, in
their uses and their compounds, suggest the international
character of fame and exile in the heroic and elegiac
poetry.
Cpds.: wīd-cūþ "famous," -ferhþ, -floga, -scofen, -wegas.
(41)

117. dēaþ (m.) "DEATH"; dēad (adj.) "DEAD."

It is remarkable that an OE ancestor of ModE DIE, which
should have been dīegan, does not occur in OE texts. The
(Germanic) word may simply not have existed in OE, and
have been borrowed in MidE from Scand. Steorfan, sweltan
forþ-gān, ge-wītan, etc., did service for it. ModG cognates are Tod, tot "death, dead."
Cpds.: dēaþ-bedd, -cwalu, -cwealm, -dæg, -fǣge, -scua,
-wērig, -wīc; gūþ-, wæl-, wundor-dēaþ. (40)

118. þurh (prep.) "THROUGH, because of."

Common as a prefix. Cognate ModG durch "through." The
emphatic stress developed a variant form þuruh in OE, the
ancestor of ModE THOROUGH (cf. burh and borough, sorg and
sorrow, mearh and marrow); the lighter ordinary stress
permitted metathesis of the r and the u. A related sb.
þyrel "pierced place" gives us (with nos- "nose") nos-
tril; a related OE verb þyrlian is the ancestor of ModE
THRILL in its old sense, "to pierce."

Cpds.: þurh-brecan, -drīfan, -dūfan, -etan, -fōn, -tēon, -wadan. (40)

119. ğeong (adj.) "YOUNG" (superl. "most recent"); ğeoguþ (f.) "YOUTH, band of young retainers."

The ğeoguþ is the young counterpart of the duguþ in a company of warriors. Cognate are ModG jung, Jugend "young, youth"; Lat. iuventa, iuvencus, iuvenis "youth, young man or bullock, young." Cpd.: ğeogoþ-feorh. (39)

120. lēoht (n., adj.) "LIGHT"; līexan (I) "shine"; līeğ (m.) "flame, fire"; lēoma (wk.m.) "light, gleam."

Cognate are Gk. lychnos, leykos "light, shining"; Lat. lūx, lucēre, lumen, lūcus, luna, lucidus "light, to shine, lamp, grove, moon, lucid"; ModG Licht(en), Leucht(en) "(to) light." "Light" in the sense "of little weight" (ModG leicht, OE lēoht) has a separate etymology. ModE gleam is not related to lēoma, but is a mnemonic aid. Like ecg, lēoma is used metonymically for the glitterer, the sword. Cpds.: æfen-, fȳr-, morgen-lēoht; līğ-draca, -eğesa, -ȳþ, æled-, beado-, byrne-, hilde-lēoma. (39)

121. metan (æ, ǣ, e) (5) "METE, measure, traverse"; ğe-met (n.) "measure, means, power" (adj.) "proper, MEET"; metod (m.) "the Measurer, God, fate"; [mǣte (adj.) "small, moderate, inferior."]

Cognate are ModG Mass, messen "measure, to measure"; Gk. medimnos "measure (of grain)"; Lat. modius, meditāri, modus "bushel, to meditate, measure/manner." Probably the group is ultimately cognate with Lat. mētēri "to MEASURE" and its numerous derivatives, and with OE mǣl "occasion, MEAL," but the latter word is not counted here. *Mōtan (No. 102) may also be related. Me(o)tod originally meant "what is meted out, fate" (cf. weird), and later, "God." Cpds.: eald-metod; metod-sceaft "decree of fate"; un-ğe-mete; un-iğmetes. (39)

122. nīþ (m.) "malice, enmity, violence, persecution, combat."

Not a nice word, but a Beowulfian word. Cognate is ModG
Neid "envy, rancor," which gives the original sense. In
cpds., often synonymous with gūþ, hilde-, etc.
Cpds.: nīþ-draca, -gæst, -ģeweorc, -grim, -heard,
-hēdiġ, -sele, -wundor; bealo-, fǣr-, here-, hete-,
inwit-, searo- "crafty," wæl-nīþ. (39)

123. (ģe-)beorgan (ea, u, o) (3) "protect, save"; ģe-
beorg (n.) "defense, protection"; burg/burh (byriġ) (f.)
"stronghold, walled town, BURG"; [byrġan (I) "BURY";
ģe-byrġa (wk.m.) "protector, surety."]

The group is apparently unconnected with beorg "hill,
BARROW" (No. 217), which is itself not connected with
bearwe "BARROW," as in wheel-barrow, cognate with beran
(No. 12). ModE BORROW is derived from beorgan, with the
idea of giving security transferred to the idea of taking the loan for which security is given. ModG cognates
are Burg, borgen, verbergen, burgen "fortress, to borrow,
to conceal, to guarantee."
Cpds.: be-, ymb-beorgan; frēo-, freoðo-, hēa-, hlēo-,
hord-, lēod-, mǣġ-, scield-burh; burh-loca, -stede,
-ware, -wela; lēod-ģebyrġea. (38)

124. hēr (adv.) "HERE"; hider (adv.) "HITHER"; heonan
(adv.) "HENCE."

Cognate are ModG hier "here," hin, hierher "hither" and
Lat. hi-c, ci-trā "here, on this side" (the suffix of
citrā corresponds to the -der of hider). The group is
related to the originally demonstrative Germanic stem
*hi- (IE *ki-) which gives us the personal pronouns,
"he," etc., not counted in this list. For the -ce ending of "hence," cf. þonan "thence." The -s sound
spelled -ce derives from an adverbial ending in MidE
(orig. a gen. sg.) seen in toward/towards; night/nights
("he plays at night" = "he plays nights").
Cpd.: hin-fūs "eager to get away." (38)

125. land (n.) "LAND."

An old Germanic form, spelled the same way (with the
variant lond) in all the Germanic langs. except pre-
Modern German (lant).
Cpds.: land-būend, -fruma, -ģemyrče, -ģeweorc, -riht,
-waru, -weard; ēa-, el-, īġ-lond. (38)

126. lāþ (adj.) "hostile, hateful, LOATHed."

Cognate with ModG Leid "distress"; Gk. aleitēs "wicked man"; borrowed from the Germanic root is French laid "ugly."
Cpds.: lāþ-bite, -ǧetēona, -līċ. (38)

127. mæðel (n.) "council, meeting"; maðelian (II) "make a (formal) speech"; (ǧe-)mǣlan (I) "make a (formal) speech"; [mǣl (n.) "speech."]

Twenty-six times in Beowulf and twice in Maldon we have the formulaic expression "X maðelode": the formula always constitutes the first half of the line; frequently X is a proper name; the verb occurs in our texts only in these poems, and only in this situation. Mǣlan is likewise formulaically used: in our texts it occurs (thrice) only in Maldon, only in the second half of the verse, always in the formula "wordum mǣlde"--"he spoke in words." The group as a whole is poetic; its words are rarely found in prose.
Cpds.: mæðel-stede, -word. (38)

128. secg (m.) "man, warrior."

The presumed cognates, Lat. sequor, socius "I follow, companion," Gk. aosseō "I help," suggest the original sense "follower, retainer." The word is found only in poetry (where it is a homophone of secg "sword," another poetic word used only once in Beowulf). It is odd that the Beowulf poet made no compounds of this frequent poetic word.
Cpd.: sele-secg. (38)

129. sorg (f.) "SORROW, distress"; [sorgian II "SORROW, grieve."]

Cognate with ModG Sorge "sorrow."
Cpds.: sorg-ċeariǧ, -ful, -lēas, -lēoþ, -lufu, -wylm; hyǧe-, inwit-, þeǧn-sorh. (38)

130. weorþ (n.) "WORTH, value, treasure" (adj.) "valued, dear"; (ǧe-)weorðian (II) "honor, exalt, adorn"; -weorðung (f.) "ornament, honor"; [wierðe (adj.) "worthy (of), entitled to."]

Cognate with ModG Wert, würdig, "worth, worthy." The weak verb weorðian is easily confused with the much more frequent strong verb weorðan "become" (No. 23). Weorðian has the sense "make worthy," esp. by splendid decoration: an object is ge-weorðod with gold.
Cpds.: weorþ-ful, -līce, -mynd; fyrd-, hord-wyrðe; brēost-, hām-, hord-, hring-, wīg-weorðung; wīg-geweorðad. (38)

131. windan (a, u, u) (3) "WIND, move fast, circle round, twist, wave" (ppl.) wunden "twisted (as of ornamentation)"; [ge-windan (3) "go, turn"; wandian (II) "turn aside, flinch"]; (ge-)wendan (I) "turn, go, WEND, change."

The pret. of wendan gradually became the pret. of "go," WENT. ModE WANDER is from the same etymon, as are ModG winden, wenden, Wandel "to wind, to turn, change." The ppl. can be confused with wund "injury, wound."
Cpds.: æt-, be-, on-windan; wunden-feax, -hals, -mæl, -stefna; on-wendan. (38)

132. (ge-)cweðan (cwæþ, cwǣdon, cweden) (5) "say, speak"; -cwide (m.) "speech" (prefix or suffix).

Quoth is archaic now, but we retain the verb in bequeath. Quote and quota are from a separate root, borrowed directly from Lat.
Cpds.: ā-, on-cweðan; æfter-cweðende; cwide-giedd; gegn-, gilp-, hlēoðor-, lār-, word-cwide. (37)

133. (ge-)feallan (ēo, ēo, ea) (7) "FALL"; (ge-)fiellan (I) "FELL, kill"; fiell (m.) "fall, slaughter."

The two verbs are related by i-umlaut, the latter the "causative" of the former (cf. sittan/settan No. 60, sīðian/sendan No. 35). The OE noun fiell was driven out in MidE by fall, based on the verb. Cognate with ModG fallen, Fall "to fall, instance."
Cpds.: ā-, be-feallan; hrā-, wæl-fiell; fyl-wērig. (37)

134. fricgan (defective: ppl. ge-frægen) (5) "ask"; ge-fricgan (5) "learn (by inquiry), hear tell"; ge-frǣge (n.) "report, hearsay"; frignan (æ, u, u) (3) "ask"; ge-frignan (3) "learn (by inquiry)."

A group which reflects the oral character of the tradi-
tional poetry. Forms of friĝnan often occur without the
ĝ. The two verbs rise from the same PrimG root; their
perfective sense is distinct and more frequent, as an
epic formula of authority (the poet reports what he hears
tell), than the simple verbs. Cognate are the Lat.
precāre, poscere, postulāre "to pray, to demand, to request"; ModG fragen, forschen "to ask, to investigate."
Cpds.: fela-fricgende. (37)

135. lǣtan (ē, ē, ǣ) (7) "LET, allow, cause to"; [lǣt
(adj.) "sluggish, slow"; lata (wk.m.) "sluggard"; (ĝe-)
lettan (I) "hinder."]

Cognate are Gk. lēdein "to be weary"; Lat. lassus, laxus
"weary, loose"; French laisser "to allow"; ModG lassen,
lass "to let, weary." The original sense seems to be to
permit something to go, through weariness or laziness.
LATE and LAZY are kindred words. In colloquial ModE the
verb lettan is preserved (as adj. and sb.) in tennis, to
describe the net's hindering the ball from free flight;
we also have the legal jargon: "without let or hindrance." Since let "hinder" practically opposes in meaning let "allow," it is not difficult to see why the
former verb was let go, when the distinct OE verbs fell
together in sound and spelling.
Cpds.: ā-, for- "leave," of-, on-lǣtan; hild-lata. (37)

136. līðan (lāþ, lidon, liden) (1) "go (esp. by water),
sail, traverse"; līðend (m.) "sea-farer"; [lid (n.)
"ship"; lida (wk.m.) "sailor, ship"; (ĝe-)lād (f.) "way,
course"]; lǣdan (I) "LEAD, bring."

As their compounds show, līðan and lād often refer to
sea-passage. The ModE words LOAD and LODE both derive
from lād, with specialized meanings (the former influenced by lade "lode" < OE hladan; the latter a vein of
ore, from a sense of a course of metal running through
the earth). Cognate is ModG leiten "to lead."
Cpds.: brim-, heaþo-, mere-, sǣ- "sailor," wǣĝ-līðend;
lid-mann; sǣ-, ȳþ-lida; brim-, lagu-, sǣ-, ȳþ-lād;
fen-ĝelād; for-lǣdan. (37)

137. (ĝe-)sellan (sealde) (I) "give, give up, offer."

Sellan does not mean SELL: the commercial sense is rare
in OE, and never occurs in our texts. The original Germanic sense is to offer, as a sacrifice. (37)

138. <u>weallan</u> (ēo, ēo, ea) (7) "WELL, surge, boil"; <u>wielm</u> (m.) "welling, surging, flood, turmoil"; <u>wǣl</u> (m.) "ocean, deep pool."

<u>Weallan</u> and <u>wielm</u> are used metaphorically of surging emotions in the breast, as if the passions were thought of as liquid humours. The root sense is probably "to roll"; hence <u>wǣl</u> (used of whirlpools as well as of deep waters in general) and WALLOW are probably connected, and the Lat. <u>volvere</u> "to roll"; Gk. <u>eilō</u> "I roll." Certainly cognate are ModG <u>wallen</u>, <u>wellen</u> "to bubble, to wave." <u>Wǣl</u> occurs only once in our texts, in a cpd.; it is distinct from <u>wǣl</u> "slaughter," a frequent word. Cpds.: brēost-, brin-, bryne-, cear-, fȳr-, heaðo-, holm-, sǣ-, sorg-wylm; wǣl-rāp. (37)

139. <u>beorn</u> (m.) "warrior, man, hero."

<u>Beorn</u> may be etym. related to <u>bearn</u> "child, son," with which it is easily confused in any case, or it may be a poetic metaphor whose original sense, "bear," was lost. The phonetically corresponding Icelandic word means "bear" exclusively. (The OED observes that OE <u>eofor</u> "boar" has an Icelandic cognate which means "warrior, man" exclusively.) <u>Beorn</u> is found only in poetry; about one-quarter of its occurrences in OE are in our texts. Cpds.: gūþ-beorn; beorn-cyning. (36)

140. <u>fāg/fāh</u> (adj.) "decorated, variegated, shining, stained."

Easy to confuse with its homophone and homograph <u>fāh/fāg</u> "hostile, guilty" (No. 146); in fact the words cannot be distinguished in some cases. Cognate with Gk. <u>poikilos</u> "parti-colored." The word bears connotations of ornate workmanship, of the dazzling, or of liquid staining: gold plating or Roman stone-work is <u>fāg</u>. Thirty-four of the occurrences, and all the cpds. in our texts, are in <u>Beowulf</u>. Cpds.: bān-, blōd-, brūn-, drēor-, <u>gold-</u>, gryre-, searo-, sinc-, stān-, swāt-, wǣl-, wyrm-fāg. (36)

141. <u>grim(m)</u> (adj.) "fierce, savage, cruel, GRIM"; <u>grimme</u> (adv.) "cruelly, terribly"; <u>gram</u> (adj.) "fierce, wrathful, hostile"; [<u>ğe-gremian</u> (I) "enrage."]

The ModE "grim" is usually not fierce enough to translate its ancestor. The formula "grim ond grǣdiğ," used

twice in Beowulf to describe Grendel and his mother, is especially fearsome sounding and memorable.
Cpds.: heaðo-, heoro-, nīþ-, searo-grim; grim-līč; æfen-from; grom-heort, -hȳdig. (36)

142. heaðu- "battle, war."

A poetic word found very rarely outside of compounds and proper names in the Germanic langs. There are 21 different compound words in our texts which begin with heaðu-. The other bases (setting aside affixes such as ge-, in-, for-, etc.) which form more than twenty compound words in our texts are gūþ (32), wæl (30), hilde (25), sǣ (21)--these four, with heaðu-, always as the first element--and mōd (22), here (21), sele (21), and wīg (21)--as either the first or the last element. (These are counts of separate forms; many occur more than once in our texts. Gūþ, for example, the poetic word par excellence, occurs 30 times in its simple form; its 32 compounds occur 53 times in Beowulf, and 3 more times in the poems in Pope's text.) These nine words may be considered the favorite words in the poetry; six of them refer to battle. Other words which vary with gūþ that have appeared in this list are nīþ, beadu, bealu. Interesting studies of poetic compounding may be found in A. G. Brodeur, The Art of Beowulf (1959), Ch. I and App. B.
Cpds.: heaðo-byrne, -dēor, -fȳr, -grim, -lāc, -lind, -līðend, -mǣre, -rǣs, -rēaf, -rinc, -rōf, -scearp, -sīoc, -stēap, -swāt, -sweng, -torht, -wǣd, -weorc, -wylm. (36)

143. lēas (adj.) "devoid of, without" (suffix) "-LESS"; [for-lēosan (-lēas, -luron, -loren) (2) "LOSE"; līesan (I) "liberate, redeem"]; losian (II) "be lost, escape."

ModE LOSS and LOOSE are derived from the etymon of this group, and LEASE "untrue," from an idea of loose in conduct. LOSE changes from the intransitive OE losian to its present transitive sense, and presumably is pronounced to rhyme with "shoes" instead of with "chose"--as it should be pronounced by normal development--because of association with LOOSE, itself directly borrowed from the Old Norse cognate of lēas. The forms of for-lēosan with r show the operation of Verner's Law (cf. čēosan, drēosan), hence ModE FORLORN. Cognate are ModG los, verlieren "loose, to lose," Gk. lyein "to loosen," Lat. luere, so-lv-ere "to free, to loosen/dissolve."
Cpds.: lēas-scēawere; dōm-, drēam- ealdor-, ende-, feoh-, feormend-, frēond-, grund-, hlāford-, sāwol-, sige-, sorh-, tīr-, þēoden-, wine-, wyn-lēas; ā-, on-līesan. (36)

144. searu (n.) "contrivance, artifice, device, skill, armor"; sierwan (I) "plot, deceive, ambush."

A word of admirable or of dastardly connotation: the reference is to the cunning machinations of the metal-smith or the elaborate artifice of a traitor. Some authorities think that the etymon is cognate with Gk. eirō "I arrange in order, I string (as a necklace)," Lat. sero, seriēs "to join in a row, row or series or chain."
Cpds.: searo-bend, -fāh, -gim(m), -grim, -hæbbend, -net(t), -nīþ, -þonc, -wundor; fyrd-, gūþ-, inwit-searo; be-syrwan. (36)

145. þēah (adv., conj.) "(al)THOUGH, however."

Cognate with ModG doch "though." (36)

146. fāh/fāg (adj.) "hostile, inimical, feuding"; fǣhþ(u) (f.) "FEUD, enmity, battle."

ModE "feud" derives from an Old French word derived from an old German word from the same root as fǣhþu. ModE FOE is from the same group; cognate also are ModG Fehde "feud," Gk. pikros "bitter" (or pikros may be related to fāg/fāh No. 140).
Cpds.: nearo-fāh; wæl-fǣhþ. (36)

147. rīċe (n.) "kingdom, realm" (adj.) "powerful"; [rīcsian (II) "rule."]

The ModE cognate "rich" is a "false friend": the OE rīċe connotes "power" without necessary reference to wealth. ModG Reich, as "The Third Reich." The Germanic root (Gothic reiks) is thought to be cognate with the Lat. rēx "king" by direct derivation via the Celtic rīx "king"--this is unlike the usual, more ancient relation of OE to Lat. words, in which both derive from a conjectural IE ancestor. If, as seems plausible but is uncertain, rēx is related to Lat. rĕgere "to rule," then rīċe is cognate with OE riht "right" (No. 203--the words are grouped separately in this list). A suffix -rīċ from this group is preserved only in bishopric. The ModE "riches" has no singular because it was originally not a plural, but borrowed from the French singular word richesse "wealth," itself borrowed from a German (Frankish) word.
Cpds.: cyne-, heofon-, weorold-rīċe. (35)

148. rinc (m.) "man, warrior."

A strictly poetic word. The cpd. hilde-rinc occurs ten
times in our texts; a favorite formula is "hār hilde-
rinc." The word may be related to OE ranc "strong,
proud" (which does not occur in our texts), and more
distantly to the riht group (No. 203), but the relations
are uncertain. The poets needed words with a variety of
initials to say "warrior" (rinc, hæleþ, wīg̊end, beorn,
secg) or "man" (mann, guma, frece, eorl, ealdor, þeg̊n,
feorh, mǣg̊, æðeling, lēod); these words have separate
histories and distinct shades of meaning, but the poets,
esp. in cpds., suppressed any very fine discriminations
of sense for the sake of alliteration. If you want to
compose alliterative poetry orally, first acquire a
tongue-tip treasury of variants for the terms "sea,
battle, man, weapon, mind, treasure, distress, land,
people and family, lord, to do, to say, to go, to know."
Cpds.: beado-, fierd-, gūþ-, hilde- "battle warrior,"
heaðo-, here-, mago-, sǣ-rinc. (35)

149. sinc (n.) "treasure, ornament."

A word found only in poetry, of unknown ancestry and
without a Modern reflex. Sinc is recorded only once as
the second element of a compound (not in our texts): its
poetic frequency depends on its usefulness in making
compounds which alliterate.
Cpds.: sinc-fæt "precious cup," -fāg, -g̊estrēon, -g̊ifa
"treasure-giver," -māððum, -þegu (sinc-fæt and sinc-g̊ifa
each occur four times). (35)

150. fēond (m.) "enemy, FIEND."

The OE verb *fēogan/*fēon "hate," of which fēond was
originally the pres. part., does not occur in our texts.
Fēond is one of the "agent nouns" like g̊ōddōnd, hettend,
āgend, hǣlend, wealdend, wīg̊end, frēond "benefactor,
enemy, owner, savior, ruler, warrior, friend"--all masculine nouns derived from the pres. part. of the Germanic
etymons of the corresponding verbs. The sense "devil" of
OE fēond is common, but it became the unique meaning only
later. Cognate with ModG Feind "devil" and perhaps with
Gk. pēma "distress," Lat. patī "to suffer" (> PASSION).
Cpds.: fēond-grāp, -scaða, -scipe. (34)

151. <u>niht</u> (f.) "NIGHT."

Cognate with Gk. <u>nyx</u>, Lat. <u>nox</u>, ModG <u>Nacht</u> "night."
Cpds.: niht-bealu, -helm, -long, -scua, -wacu, -weorc;
middel-, sin-niht. (34)

152. <u>swīþ</u> (adj.) "strong, harsh, right (hand)"; <u>swīðe</u>
(adv.) "very, quite, strongly, severely"; [<u>ofer-swīðan</u>
(I) "over-power."]

The adverb often has a merely emphatic sense. The word
<u>sound</u> (healthy, strong) may be related (OE <u>sund</u>), but
the words are not joined in this list. Cognate is ModG
<u>geschwind</u> "quick."
Cpds.: swīþ-ferhþ, -hicgende, -mōd; þrȳþ-swȳþ; un-swīðe.
(34)

153. (n)<u>āgan</u> (āh/āg, āhst, āhte) (pret.-pres.) "have,
possess, OWN"; [<u>āgen</u> (adj.) "OWN"; <u>āgend</u> (m.) "owner"];
<u>æht</u> (f.) "property, control."

The post-OE history of this verb resembles that of other
pret.-pres. verbs, in that the pret. subjunctive (āhte)
came to be felt as a separate verb in the MidE period,
whence ModE "OUGHT" as distinct from "owe." The ModE
"own" has developed from pret. forms, keeping the original meaning, but the direct reflex of the infinitive,
OWE, has altered the OE sense. Cognate with ModG <u>eigen</u>,
Eigentum "to own, property."
Cpds.: āgend-frēa; blǣd-, bold-, folc-, mægen-āgende;
gold-, māðm-æht. (33)

154. (<u>ge-</u>)<u>fōn</u> (fēng, fēngon, fangen) (7) "seize, grasp";
<u>feng</u> (m.) "grasp, grip."

ModE FANG, the grasper, is the obvious mnemonic aid.
Cognate are ModG <u>fangen</u> "to seize" (with frequent cpds.
in <u>ge-</u>, <u>emp-</u>, <u>an-</u>) and Lat. <u>pactum</u>, <u>pāx</u> "pact, peace"--a
peace being a compact with one's enemies, and a pact
being a thing secured--Gk. <u>paktoō</u> "I fasten." The OE
<u>fǣger</u> "fair" may be related, but the words are kept sepa-
rate in this list. <u>Feng</u> is what Beowulf has plenty of.
Cpds.: be-, <u>on-</u> "seize," þurh-, wiþ-, ymbe-fōn; inwit-
feng. (33)

155. oþþe (conj.) "OR."

It is not certain that "or" is a direct reflex of oþþe,
with a final r somehow added in the 12th c. (cf. the
cognate ModG oder "or," with similarly inexplicable r
ending.) (33)

156. sōþ (adj.) "true" (sb.n.) "truth"; sōðe (adv.)
"truly"; [sēðan (I) "declare (the truth)"]; syn(n) (f.)
"SIN, wrong-doing"; synniġ (adj.) "SINful"; synnum (adv.)
"guiltily"; [ġe-synġian (II) "SIN."]

Like cūþ (no. 33), sōþ (ModE SOOTH) is derived from an
earlier form *sonþ-, from which the n preceding the dental was lost, and the vowel lengthened "in compensation."
This earlier form more closely resembles the cognate
forms, Lat. sontis (gen. sg. of sons) "guilty" and ModG
Sünde "sin," as well as the OE cognate synn. The idea of
the true and the idea of the guilty are related through
the idea of emphatically being the one. So the group is
etym. related to forms of the verb "to be," like OE sint
(not counted here), ModG sind, Lat. sunt "they are." The
relationship of "being" and "guilt" is still present,
even outside of the work of Kafka, as was demonstrated
by a comedian who, a long time ago, played upon a poli-
tician's motto, "Nemo's the one," by hinting that the
meaning was not that Nemo would be victorious, but that
he is guilty. The prefix syn- is easily confused with
its homograph prefix syn-/sin-, meaning "continually,
great." For instance, syn-scaða may mean "sinful harmer"
or "great harmer." To SOOTHE has developed its meaning
from "to assuage Nemo by asserting that what Nemo says
is true (sōþ)," i.e. to be a yes-man, from OE sōðian
(not in our texts). A sooth-sayer is not soothing.
Cpds.: sōþ-cyning, -fæst, -ġiedd, -līċe; syn-bysiġ,
-scaða (?); un-synniġ; un-synnum. (33)

157. wǣpen (n.) "WEAPON"; [wǣpnan (I) "arm."]

The ModG Luftwaffe may precisely be translated "air
force," since Waffe, like its OE cognate wǣpen, has a
general sense "force" as well as a particular sense
"weapon."
Cpds.: hilde-, siġe-wǣpen; wǣpen-ġewrixl; wǣpned-monn.
(33)

158. frætwe (f. pl.) "ornaments, decorated armor,
treasure"; [frætwan (I) "adorn"; ġe-frætwian (II)

"adorn"; g̊eatwa/g̊etawa (f. pl.) "equipment, precious
objects."]

Of course you know the good ModE word TAW meaning "prepare, adorn" (ModE TOOL is cognate); these words are
formed on it, with the prefix for- in its stressed form
(fræ + tawa > frǣtwa) and the prefix g̊e- (g̊etawa, g̊eatwa).
The words mean practically the same thing, and bespeak
the high respect which Germanic peoples had for good
craftmanship, esp. armor and weaponry. Perhaps cognate
with Lat. bonus "good" (Old Latin duenos) and another
ModE word, TOW ("hemp").
Cpds.: ēored-, gryre-, hilde-g̊eatwa; wīg̊-, gūþ-g̊etawa;
here-g̊eatu (all these compounds present forms of the same
word); g̊eato-līč. (32)

159. frēa (wk.m.) "lord, king, God."

Perhaps cognate with the name of the Norse goddess of
love, Freyja, and perhaps also with the for group (No. 11),
as the chief is the foremost.
Cpds.: āgend-, līf-, sin-frēa; frēa-drihten, -wine,
-wrāsn. (32)

160. g̊if (conj.) "IF."

Cognate with ModG ob "whether." The word is not the
imperative of g̊iefan "give" ("let it be granted that" as
to mean "if") as its spelling in Gothic (ibai, jabai)
shows: Gothic for "to give" is giban. (32)

161. sceaða/scaða (wk.m.) "foe, harmer, warrior"; (g̊e-)
sceþþan (scōd, scōdon, sceaðen) (6) (also I) "harm,
injure, SCATHE."

The most familiar words from this group in ModE are un-
SCATHED, SCATHing. Our pronunciation with the initial
sk sound reveals that the English word was probably borrowed from the Scand. equivalent (Old Norse skaða)
rather than directly from the OE (cf. skirt/shirt, from
Scand. and OE). Cognate with ModG Schaden "harm," prob.
with Gk. askēthēs "unscathed."
Cpds.: attor-, dol-, fǣr-, fēond-, gūþ-, hearm-, hell-,
lēod-, mān- "wicked foe," scyn-, syn-, þēod-, ūht-scaða.
(32)

162. geador (adv.) "toGETHER"; -gædere (adv.) "together, jointly"; [gædeling (m.) "kinsman, companion"]; ġiedd (n.) "song, tale, speech"; [ġieddian (II) "speak, discourse."]

The OE gaderian GATHER does not occur in our texts. If we imagine a speaker or scop collecting his thoughts before he composes his utterance, we can see the relation of "together" and ġiedd, but the relationship is by no means certain. The th of gather and together came into English in the MidE period, from the d. The group may be related to gōd ("fitting," hence good), but the words are kept separate in this list.
Cpds.: on-geador; æt- "together," to-gædere; cwide-, geōmor-, sōþ-, word-ġiedd. (31)

163. (ġe-)bindan (a, u, u) (3) "BIND, imprison"; ġe-bind (n.) "fastening"; bend (f.) "BOND."

The ModE words "bind, bend, band, bond" are cognate. "Band" and "bond" are variants of a cognate Scand. word, which was adopted and rivaled the OE bend in the MidE period, finally driving it out. In the sense of "company" or of "strip," "band" was borrowed into English from French, but the French words are derived also from Germanic words. OE bend is now preserved only nautically or technically, as in sheetbend, a knot which joins two lengths of rope endlong.
Cpds.: on-bindan; īs-ġebind; ancor-, fȳr-, hell-, hyġe-, īren-, searo-, sinu-, wæl-bend. (30)

164. byrne (wk.f.) "coat of mail, corselet, BYRNIE."

The word may have been borrowed by Germanic from Old Slavic, or vice versa. The ModG cognate is Brünne. With the less frequent syrce, byrne is the standard term for body armor.
Cpds.: byrn-wiga; gūþ-, heaðo-, here-, īren-, īsern-byrne. (30)

165. dæl (m.) "part, share, (good) DEAL"; [ġe-dāl (n.) "parting, separation"]; (ġe-)dǣlan (I) "distribute, share, divide, DEAL out, sever."

The ModG cognates Teil, teilen "part, to divide," with their many cpds., preserve the senses of sharing and distributing better than ModE "deal"--but ModE DOLE, derived from dāl, keeps the old meaning. Cognate with

Gk. daiomai "to share"; if a demon was originally one who,
like a beast of battle, devoured corpses, the Gk. daimon
is also cognate.
Cpds.: ealdor-, līf-ğedāl; be-dǣlan "deprive." (30)

166. hring (m.) "RING, ring-mail"; hringed (adj.) "formed
of rings."

The iron rings of which ring-mail was made were valuable
in themselves, like any metalwork. For this reason the
armor sense of the word often approaches in connotation
the meaning of the ornamental rings (bracelets and neck-
laces) which lords dispensed to their thanes. Cognate
with ModG Ring, Gk. kirkos, Lat. circus "ring."
Cpds.: hring-boga, -īren, -loca, -mǣl, -naca, -net,
-sele, -þegu, -weorðung; bān-hring; hringed-stefna. (30)

167. līč (n.) "body, form, LIKEness, corpse"; -līč
(general adjectival suffix) "-LIKE, -LY"; -līče (adv.
suffix) "-LY"; [līca (wk.m.) "LIKEness"; līč-ness (f.)
"LIKENESS"]; ge-līč (adj.) "(a)LIKE"; [līčian (II)
"please, be pleasing."]

Not counted here are the numerous words with the suffixes
-līč, -līče (although these cpds. are counted in the
groups to which the other element belongs), except when
-līč means "figure, likeness." Our "to LIKE" derives
from līčian, which originally must have meant "to be con-
formable," hence pleasant. During the MidE period the
impersonal idiom "it likes me" (it pleases me) was altered
into the Modern "I like it"; cf. methinks/I think. Cognate are ModG gleich "like" (cf. ge-līč), Leiche "corpse."
Cpds.: eofor-, swīn-līč; līč-sār, -syrce, -hama "body"
(the garment of flesh; cf. flǣsc-hama); wyrm-līca;
on-līčness. (30)

168. (ge-)sprecan (æ, ǣ, e) (5) "SPEAK, say"; sprǣč
(f.) "SPEECH."

The r began to drop from the verb in LWS: the Beowulf MS
has one example. Cognate with ModG sprechen, Sprache
"to speak, speech," more distantly with Lat. spargere "to
strew" (cf. SPARKLE, diSPERSE), which points to an original root meaning "move quickly": speech is a scattering
of words.
Cpds.: ǣfen-, ğylp-sprǣč. (30)

169. ȳþ (f.) "wave."

By metonymy, esp. in cpds., the word often means sea; by metaphor, it refers to surges of flame or sorrow (cf. wielm No. 138). Possibly related to the wæter group (No. 187).
Cpds.: ȳþ-ğeblond, -ğewinn, -lād, -lāf, -lida; flōd-, līğ-, sealt-, wæter-ȳþ. (30)

170. bealu (n.) "evil, malice, misery, BALE"; [bealu (adj.) "baleful, evil, pernicious."]

The word is quite distinct from OE bǣl "fire, funeral pyre," but the two words have been confused in MidE and ModE, as hell-fire is baleful. Bealu is only rarely found in prose; the noun was originally the n. of the adj.
Cpds.: bealo-cwealm, -hycgende, -hȳdiğ, -nīþ, -sīþ, -ware; cwealm-, ealdor-, feorh- "mortal affliction," hreþer-, lēod-, morðor-, niht-, sweord-, wīğ-bealu. (29)

171. ēac (adv.) "also" (prep.) "in addition to"; ēacen (adj.) "great, pregnant"; (ğe-)weaxan (ēo, ēo, ea) (7) "grow, WAX"; wæstm (m.) "growth, fruit, form."

Chaucer commonly used eke "also"; we have it in the verb form "to eke out," to augment. The cognates are Gk. ayxein, Lat. augēre "to increase," ModG wachsen, Wachstum "to grow, growth." From augēre may come augur, "one who predicts (increased) fortune." The adj. ēacen is the past participle of a verb obsolete in OE. The verb wax has been almost driven out by the use in ModE of its synonym "grow," except in reference to phases of the moon. (Some doubt the relation of ēac to the other words in this group.)
Cpds.: un-weaxen; ēacen-cræftiğ; here-wæstm. (28)

172. gār (m.) "spear."

Rarely found in prose. The PrimG conjectured ancestor *gaizo- has rare confirmation in the Lat. borrowing gaesum "javelin (such as the Gauls use)," Gk. gaison. Kin to gār are ModE GARlic, GARfish, and GORE, the triangular piece cut from a skirt to narrow it at the waist. The seam made from joining the sides of a gore is a "dart," from a French word meaning the same thing as gār. The shape of the head of the spear suggested these sartorial terms. The word gār-secg "sea" is

obscure in etymology, and is not counted here (it occurs three times in Beowulf), but it may be related.
Cpds.: gār-berend, -cēne, -cwealm, -holt, -mittung, -rǣs, -wiga, -wīġend; bon-, frum-gār. (28)

173. -ġietan (ea, ēa, ie) (5) "grasp"; be-ġietan (5) "GET"; [for-ġietan (5) "FORGET"]; on-ġietan (5) "perceive, understand"; [ēþ-beġēte (adj.) "easy to get."]

The base verb is found only in cpds. Cognate with ModG vergessen "to forget"; Lat. praeda, praehendere "booty, to grasp"; Gk. chandanein "to hold." Our verbs GET, forGET, beGET are from the Old Norse cognates. The sense "perceive" is like our colloquial "get it" (cf. "catch on, comprehend"); GUESS is derived from the same group with a similar semantic idea. (28)

174. hēah (adj.) "HIGH, deep, exalted."

Like Lat. altus, hēah can mean "deep" when applied to the sea ("the high sea"). It often bears a noble connotation in OE, as now ("high art"). Esp. in its acc. sg. form and in its wk. forms (hēanne, hēan) the word is easily confused with the unrelated adj. hēan "contemptible, base." Cognate with ModG hoch "high." As often, the final fricative sound of the word was lost in pronunciation, beginning with the 14th c., but retained in the spelling (cf. though, through, etc.).
Cpds.: hēah-burh, -cyning, -fæder, -ġesceap, -ġestrēon, -lufu, -sele, -setl, -stede. (28)

175. here (m.) "army, (in cpds.) war."

The ModE HARRY and HARROW both derive from the verb herian/herġian (wk. II), based on this noun but not found in our texts. Christ did not "rake," but he "plundered" hell, as an army plunders a countryside, when he harrowed it. The homophonic ModE harrow "rake" is not related. Likewise the homophonic OE verb herian (wk.I) "praise" is unrelated. A HARBOR is a here-beorg, a shelter for (or from) an army. The -er- changes to -ar- as in bark, barrow, marsh, hart (cf. the British pronunciation of clerk, sergeant, Hertford, Berkeley, etc.). The HERIOT is the here-ġeatu, the "army equipment" a tenant owes his lord. Cognate are ModG Heer "army," Gk. koiranos "military commander." The word varies with gūþ, wīġ, hilde, etc., in the poetry, providing a convenient initial for alliteration.

Cpds.: here-brōga, -byrne, -flīema, -ģeatu, -grīma, -lāf, -net, -nīþ, -pad, -rinc, -sceaft, -spēd, -strǣl, -syrce, -wǣd, -wæstm, -wīsa; æsc-, flot-, scip-, sin-here. (28)

176.: lȳtel (adj.) "LITTLE"; lǣssa (comp.) "LESS"; lǣsest (superl.) "LEAST"; lȳt (n. indeclinable) "little, small number" (adv.) "little, not at all"; lǣs (comp.) "LESS, lest"; [lȳtlian (II) "grow less, diminish."]

Probably connected with LOUT (< OE lūtan) meaning "bow down."
Cpds.: un-lȳtel; lȳt-hwōn. (28)

177. nēah (adv., prep.) "near, NIGH"; nēan (adv.) "from near, near"; (ģe-)nǣģan (I) "approach, address, attack.

The comp. (nēar) and superl. (nīehsta) of nēah > ModE NEAR and NEXT; the former drove out NIGH, now archaic. Cognate with ModG nah, nahen "near, to approach." (28)

178. sefa (wk.m.) "mind, heart, spirit."

The Middle High German beseben means "to perceive," so the original reference of the noun may be to a faculty of cognition rather than a physical organ; perhaps cognate with Lat. sapere, sapor "to perceive, taste." Remember that the intervocalic f is voiced to sound like v. Cpd.: mōd-sefa (sefa occurs 18 times, mōd-sefa 10). (28)

179. þīn (possessive adj.) "THINE, THY."

The second person sg. possessive adj., originally the genitive of the pronoun þū "THOU," but taking strong adj. case endings (cf. mīn No. 41). Cognate with ModG dein "thy," Lat. tū "thou." (28)

180. weal(l) (m.) "WALL."

Borrowed by several West Germanic langs. from the Lat. vallum, which has the military sense still preserved in ModG Wall "rampart." The West Saxon spelling shows characteristic "breaking"; in Anglian the word is spelled wall, the direct ancestor of the modern word.

Cpds.: weall-clif, -steall; bord-, eorþ-, sǣ, scild-weall. (28)

181. bana (wk.m.) "slayer, murderer"; benn (f.) "wound."

The ModE reflex is BANE.
Cpds.: bon-gār; ecg-, feorh-, gāst-, hand-, mūþ-bana;
ben-ġeat; feorh-, sex-benn. (27)

182. (ġe-)hweorfan (ea, u, o) (3) "turn, go, move about";
[hwierfan (I) "move about"]; hwyrft (m.) "turning, motion."

The OE hwearf, a cognate word not in our texts, means
"crowd" and also WHARF, both presumably from an idea of
the reciprocal, eddying movement described by hweorfan.
Cognate is ModG werben "to publicize, solicit." In "The
Seafarer" hweorfan describes the wheeling course of a mind
flying forth like a bird.
Cpds.: æt-, ġeond-, ond-, ymbe-hweorfan; ed-hwyrft. (27)

183. wundor (n.) "WONDER."

ModG Wunder is cognate. A West Germanic word of unknown
origin.
Cpds.: wundor-fæt, -bebod, -dēaþ, -līċ, -māððum, -sīon,
-smiþ; hand-, nīþ-, searo-wundor. (27)

184. wyrm (m.) "serpent, snake, WORM."

In Beowulf the dragon is called wyrm as well as draca
(the latter a Latin borrowing); in early English the word
usually refers to a larger creature than a worm. Cognate
are ModG Wurm, Lat. vermis "worm." As with OE wer/Lat.
vir, Grimm's Law does not affect the sounds of the Lat.
cognate, so it still closely resembles the English (ModE
vermin of course is borrowed from Romance). For the o
spelling of ModE "word" see cuman (No. 32) and cf. wonder,
worse, wolf, wort--all with historical u vowels.
Cpds.: wyrm-cynn, -fāh, -hord, -līca. (27)

185. heofon (m.) "HEAVEN."

Note the voiced f between vowels, which makes this word
(like ofer, lufu, etc.) closer to ModE pronunciation

than it appears. The Scand. and High German word of
equivalent meaning which appears as ModG Himmel has no
obvious relation to heofon.
Cpds.: heofon-līč, -rīče. (26)

186. slēan (slōg, slōgon, slægen) (6) "strike, SLAY";
ge-slēan (6) "achieve by striking, win"; -sleaht/-slieht
(m. or n.) "SLAUGHTER, blow."

The sens of slēan, a "contracted verb," is more often
"strike" than "slay." Cognate is ModG schlagen "to
strike." Related are ModE SLY (cunning, able to strike),
and similarly "SLEIGHT (of hand)," and "SLEDGE (hammer),"
and the weaver's SLAY, with which he strikes the weft
down.
Cpds.: be-, of-slēan; ge-, on-slieht; wæl-sleaht. (26)

187. wæter (n.) "WATER"; [wæta (wk.m.) "moisture, WET-
ness."]

Cognate with ModG Wasser, Gk. hydōr (as in hydroplane,
etc.) "water," Lat. unda "wave." WASH and OTTER are ultimately cognate, and probably winter (the wet season),
but this last (No. 206) is not a sure enough relation to
count here.
Cpds.: wæter-egesa, -ȳþ. (26)

188. folde (wk.f.) "earth, ground"; feld (m.) "FIELD."

One of the best verses in Beowulf varies and abbreviates
"fyrgenstrēam/under næssa genipu" ("a mountain-stream
under the dark places of the cliffs"). It is "flōd
under foldan," which by its linked sounds seems to reflect a link of water and earth, at Grendel's mere
(l. 1361). The ModG cognate of feld has the same spelling and meaning. The words may possibly be related to
flett "floor, hall," flōr "floor," and folm(e) "hand,"
which all occur in our texts, but the etymologies are
too uncertain for the words to be counted here.
Cpds.: fold-bold, -būend, -weg; wæl-feld. (25)

18º. īren (n.) "sword, IRON"; īren (adj.) "of iron";
īsern- "iron."

The sense "sword" appears by the familiar metonymy (cf.
hilde-lēoma, ecg, hring-mǣl, lāf, gūþ-wine). Cognate

ModG Eisen "iron": the r appears only in English, of
the Germanic and Celtic langs. in which the word is
found (the root may be related to Lat. Ira IRE). Oddly,
the more poetic OE form with r drove out the more pro-
saic OE form with s in the MidE period, whereas prose
forms usually drive out poetic ones. The r of Iren
looks like a product of Verner's Law (cf. ceosan/coren)
but it is probably not, so "the rhotacism is obscure"
(Gk. rho = r).
Cpds.: Iren-bend, -byrne, -heard, -þreat; eal-, hring-
Iren; Isern-byrne, -scur. (25)

190. twegen (m.), twa (f.), tu (n.) "TWO, TWAIN"; tweone
(be . . . tweonum) "BETWEEN"; tweo (wk.m.) "doubt";
[ge-twaeman (I) "separate"; to-twaeman (I) "divide in two"];
ge-twaefan (I) "separate"; twelf "TWELVE."

As genders lost their distinctions, the separate forms of
twegen in English became redundant, and twa (> TWO) took
over the regular uses. "Doubt" arises when two choices
are present; cf. the cognate ModG Zweifel "doubt" (ModG
zwei "two"). Twelve (Gothic twa-lif) probably means
"(with) two left (over from ten)," ModG zwölf. Cognate
with twegen are most IE words meaning "two": Gk., Lat.
duo. The OE "dual" pronouns wit, git may derive their
final t's from the "two" group.
Cpd.: bu-tu "both." (25)

191. wiht (f., n.) "creature, anything, AUGHT" (adv.)
"at all" (ne wiht = "NAUGHT, not a WHIT").

The ModE WIGHT is archaic. The ModG cognate Wicht has a
slightly diminutive sense, "creature, infant"; the cognates in other Germanic langs. often refer to demons or
elves. AUGHT, "anything at all," is from a-wiht, "ever
a whit." U.S. speakers use "ought" to mean "zero"; "an
ought" is "a nought" falsely divided, from OE nowiht,
"nothing."
Cpds.: o-, a-wiht/aht, æl-wiht. (25)

192. bord (n.) "shield."

The mnemonic connection of bord with ModE BOARD is inevi-
table; the OE word probably is a metonymic sense of the
word for "board." Or it may be a metonymic sense of a
homophone, another OE bord which had fallen into the same
gender, meaning "border, ship-BOARD, rim." The last
sense could allow the reference to "shield"--a sense of

bord found only in poetry. Probably the Anglo-Saxons
knew as little as we which word was the origin of the
poetic metonymy, because the confusion of originally
separate genders indicates that the words were beginning
to be confused in OE times. Cognate with ModG Bort
"board" or Bord "border."
Cpds.: bord-hæbbende, -hrēoða, -rand, -weall, -wudu;
hilde-, wīg-bord. (24)

193. cræft (m.) "strength, power, skill, cunning, CRAFT";
cræftig (adj.) "strong, skilled."

The ModG cognate Kraft "power" preserves the primary
sense of the word; the ModE senses of skill and cunning,
and of one's trade, are not usual in OE (and these
senses are peculiar to English of the Germanic langs.).
Cpds.: gūþ-, leoðo-, mægen-, nearo-, wīg-cræft; ēacen-,
lagu-, lēoþ-, wīg-cræftig. (24)

194. fæder (m.) "FATHER."

The classic example of Grimm's Law: Skt. pitár, Gk.
patēr, Lat. pater, Gothic fadar, ModG Vater. The medial
d changed to th in English around the 15th c.; cf. gather
hither, together, weather, with th for earlier d.
Cpds.: ær-, eald-, hēah-, wuldor-fæder; fæder-æðelu;
fæderan-mǣg; suhter-ǧefæderan. (24)

195. (ǧe-)hīeran (I) "HEAR, obey, perceive."

To hear docilely is to be apt to obey. Cognate with
ModG hören, gehören, gehorsam "to hear, to belong to,
obedient." Perhaps cognate with the scēawian group just
below. (24)

196. scēawian (II) "look at, examine, see"; [ǧe-scēawian
(II) "SHOW"; lēas-scēawere (m.) "deceitful observer,
spy"; scīene (adj.) "beautiful."]

The sense "show," even of the ǧe- prefixed verb, is rare
in OE; not until the early MidE period did the word de-
velop its modern causative meaning (cause to see = show).
Cognate are Gk. thyoskoos, koein "observer of sacrifices,
to observe"; Lat. cavēre "to beware"; ModG schauen "look."
Scīene (spelled scȳne in Beowulf)> ModE SHEEN; cognate
ModG schön "beautiful." The verb is frequent in Beowulf;

the wise warriors seem always to be looking things over carefully.
Cpd.: ğeond-scēawian. (24)

197. (ğe-)čēosan (čēas, curon, coren) (2) "CHOOSE, taste, try"; cyst (f.) "choicest one, the best, (in cpds.) picked company, virtue"; [costian (II) "try, make trial of."]

The original sense of this group involved trying out, or having a taste of something. Cognate are Gk. geysein, Lat. gustāre "to taste," ModG kosten "to try, taste." The translation of cyst as "choice," with the idea "se- lect, premium" (as in our quality-grade of meat), is happy, because the word CHOICE, borrowed by English from Old French, was ultimately derived from a Germanic rela- tive (like Gothic kausjan) of the ancestor of čēosan (Gothic kiusan). On the other hand, ModE "cost" (to have a certain price) is not Germanic in origin, but de- rived from a Latin idiom with constāre "stand at a price." Verner's Law describes the voicing of the medial s in the strong verb to z, and a regular West Germanic shift altered z to r, before OE times.
Cpds.: ēored-, gum-, hilde-cyst. (23)

198. (ğe-)drēosan (drēas, druron, droren) (2) "fall, de- cline, fail"; drēor (m., n.) "blood"; drēoriğ (adj.) "bloody, sad"; [drysmian (II) "become gloomy."]

Some scholars doubt that the two senses of drēoriğ denote the same word, but the semantic relation is easy enough. ModG cognate traurig "sad." The ModE reflex DREARY has lost the connotation of battle suffering, wounds. Blood, of course, is what falls. Possibly drūsian "stagnate" (> DROWSE) is related, but it is not counted here. Only drēosan of this group is found outside of poetry.
Cpds.: bedroren; drēor-fāh; heoro-, sāwul-, wæl-drēor; drēoriğ-hlēor; heoro-, sele-drēoriğ. (23)

199. ende (m.) "END, boundary"; [endian (II) "END."]

Cognate with ModG Ende, with the same meaning. The ulti- mate relations of the word are complex: the idea of boundary leads to the idea of the thing lying opposite, hence (perhaps) the common OE prefix and- "opposite, counter, against" (ModG ent-, a privative or negative prefix, like Lat.-ModE de- as in "defuse, decelerate, demythologize"). The conjunction and/ond and the prefix and- may be related, but the words are not counted in

64

this list. The conjunction, spelled <u>ond</u> when it is not
abbreviated with the usual mark shaped like a figure 7
("Tyronian <u>et</u>"), occurs 311 times in <u>Beowulf</u>, by
Klaeber's count. Related ultimately are Gk. <u>anti</u>
"against," Lat. <u>ante</u>, <u>anterior</u> "before, anterior."
Cpds.: ende-dæg, -dōgor, -lāf, -lēan, -lēas, -sæta,
-stæf; woruld-ende. (23)

200. <u>grund</u> (m.) "GROUND, bottom, plain, land."

Cognate with ModG <u>Grund</u> "ground," and perhaps related
to OE <u>grindan</u> "GRIND," but the verb is not counted here.
It has been suggested that the name <u>Grendel</u> is cognate,
but the derivation is disputed.
Cpds.: grund-būend, -hyrde, -lēas, -wong, -wyrġen;
eormen-, mere-, sæ-grund. (23)

201. <u>hræd-</u> (adj.) "quick, swift, hasty"; <u>hræðe</u> (adv.)
"quickly, soon."

ModE RATHER is the reflex of the comp. hræðor of hræðe,
"more quickly" > "more willingly." <u>Hræd-</u> is only found
in cpds. in our texts.
Cpds.: hræd-līċe, -wyrde. (23)

202. <u>ræd</u> (m.) "advice, counsel, help, benefit"; <u>rædan</u>
(ē, ē, æ) (7) (or wk. I) "counsel, provide for, rule,
possess"; [ġe-rædan (I) "decide"; <u>Rædend</u> (m.) "Ruler
(God)"; <u>ġe-ræd</u> (adj.) "skillful, apt."]

In ModE the archaic spelling REDE is often used for the
OE sense "give counsel," to distinguish the verb from
READ, the newer spelling of the same word, meaning "read
a text." Only English and Old Icelandic, of this common
Germanic group, have the sense "read a text," presumably
from a sense of "explain something obscure." Richard
(II) the <u>Redeless</u> and Æthelred the Un<u>ready</u> were ill-
advised kings, not tardy ones; ModE READY is more distantly related to <u>ræd</u>. <u>Rædan</u> was a "reduplicating" verb,
showing a pret. <u>rēord</u> alongside <u>rēd</u>; it coalesced in
many forms with a weak verb of similar meaning. ModG
<u>Rat</u>, <u>raten</u>, <u>gerade</u>, <u>bereit</u> "advice, to advise, direct,
ready." <u>Ræd</u> may be cognate with a number of other words,
if the IE <u>ar-1</u> group is a single etym. group: art,
inert, harmony, arms, arm, ratio, rite.
Cpds.: ræd-bora; an-, folc-, fæst-ræd; sele-, weorod-
rædend. (23)

203. riht (n.) "RIGHT, privilege, correctness" (adj.)
"right, proper"; rihte (adv.) "rightly"; [ge-rihtan (I)
"direct."]

See rīče (No. 147) and rinc (No. 148). Cognate with
ModG Recht, richtig, "right," Gk. orektos, Lat. rectus
"stretched out, straight." To make things more difficult, the word may be related to reččan "to narrate" and
racu "recounting," and, less likely and more distantly,
to reččan "to care for" and (ge-)rǣčan "to REACH." None
of these possible relations is counted here.
Cpds.: ēðel-, folc-, land-, un-, word-, upp-riht; æt-,
un-rihte; wiðer-ræhtes. (23)

204. sigor (m.) "victory"; sige- "victory, victorious,
glorious."

The prefix is frequent in a military sense; to speak of
the Cross as a sige-bēam emphasizes the paradox. Cognate
with ModG Sieg, "victory," familiar to English speakers
as part of the Nazi salute, Gk. echō "I possess."
Cpds : sige-bēam, -drihten, -ēadiğ, -folc, -hrēþ,
-hrēðiğ, -hwīl, -lēas, -rōf, -þēod, -wǣpen; sigor-ēadiğ,
-fæst; hrēþ-, wīğ-sigor. (23)

205. weorod (n.) "band of men, company, troop."

Perhaps related to OE wer "man" (No. 99) or wer(e)
"troop."
Cpds.: eorl-, flet-, heorþ-weorod; weorod-rǣdend. (23)

206. winter (n.) "WINTER, (in plural) years"; [syfan-
wintre (adj.) "seven-year-old."]

The meaning "year" persists, in poetry esp., to the
modern period. ModG Winter. See wæter (No. 187). The
cpds. reflect what the Anglo-Saxons thought of it.
Cpds.: winter-čeald, -čeariğ. (23)

207. āg-lǣca/ǣg-lǣca (wk.m.) "monster, fiend, warrior";
[āg-lǣc-wīf (n.) "female monster" (i.e., Grendel's
mother).]

Of unknown etymology; used only in poetry. In Beowulf
the word is occasionally used of men as well as monsters.
(22)

208. beorht (adj.) "BRIGHT, splendid"; [beorhte (adv.)
"brightly"; beorhtian (II) "sound clearly or loud."]

The aural sense of the verb is comparable to the sense
"battle-resounding" of heaðo-torht ("-bright") in Beowulf,
or the visual and aural senses of the Lat. argūtus "clear,
shrill." Probably from the same root is the tree-name
BIRCH (of bright bark); perhaps also breġdan "move quickly (flash), brandish"> BRAID.
Cpds.: sadol-, wlite-beorht. (22)

209. drēam (m.) "joy, festivity, noisy merriment, bliss,
music-making."

It is not certain that drēam is identical with the ancestor of the ModE DREAM. The Germanic cognates of the
latter, e.g. ModG Traum "dream," often have the sense of
"sleeping vision"; the origin of the meaning "noisy merriment," if the two words are one, is uncertain. Appar-
ent cognates of drēam in other IE langs. mean "shout."
Old Norse influence in MidE may have affected the sense
of the English word, or the OE word may have been lost
and replaced, or the sense "sleeping vision" may indepen-
dently have risen from the sense "pleasure." Studies of
the word may be found in PMLA 46 and Rev. Engl. Stud. 25.
Cpds.: drēam-healdende, -lēas; glēo-, gum-, medu-, mon-,
sele-drēam. (22)

210. eard (m.) "land, homeland, estate, country"; eardian
(II) "dwell, inhabit."

Apparently not cognate with eorðe (No. 83), but probably
cognate with Gk. aroein, Lat. arāre "to plow." The verb
"to EAR" (to plow)< OE erian survived into the ModE
period (Shakespeare).
Cpds.: eard-ġeard, -lufu, -stapa. (22)

211. flōd (m. or n.) "FLOOD, current, sea"; [flōwan (ēo,
ēo, ō) (7) "FLOW."]

Cognate with ModG Flut "flood," and with Gk. ploein "to
swim," Lat. plōrāre, pluit "to weep, it rains."
Cpds.: flōd-weġ, -ȳþ; mere-flōd. (22)

212. gāst/gǣst (m.) "soul, GHOST, demon."

Cognate with ModG G̲e̲i̲s̲t̲ "spirit, mind, sprite." The word
may originally derive from terms meaning "anger," ultimately "tear to pieces." The word is easy to confuse
with OE g̊iest "stranger, guest" (Lat. h̲o̲s̲t̲i̲s̲), which is
sometimes spelled (with a short vowel) g̲æ̲s̲t̲. GHASTly and
aGHAST are cognate.
Cpds.: ellen-, ellor- "alien spirit," g̊eōsceaft-, wæl-
gǣst; gǣst-līc̊, -bona. (22)

213. g̊eond (prep.) "through, throughout, over" (prefix)
"over, through, thoroughly."

Cognate with ModE YOND, YON, beYOND, and ModG j̲e̲n̲e̲r̲ "that
(one)."
Cpds.: g̊eond-brǣdan, -hweorfan, -scēawian, -sēon,
-þenc̊an, -wlītan. (22)

214. g̊iet(a̲) (adv.) "YET, still"; þ̲ā̲-g̊iet (adv.) "still,
further."

The anterior etymology is obscure. (22)

215. ū̲t̲ (adv.) "OUT"; ū̲t̲a̲n̲ (adv.) "from without."

Cognate with ModG a̲u̲s̲ "from, out of," Lat. u̲s̲-q̲u̲e̲"up to."
Cpds.: ūt-fūs, -weard; ūtan-weard. (22)

216. w̲u̲d̲u̲ (m.) "WOOD, tree, forest."

Often used in a transferred sense for a ship or the
Cross or a spear.
Cpds.: wudu-rēc; bǣl-, bord-, gomen-, heal-, holt-,
mæg̊en-, sǣ-, sund-, þrec-wudu. (22)

217. b̲e̲o̲r̲g̲ (m.) "hill, (grave-) mound, BARROW."

Cognate with ModG B̲e̲r̲g̲ "mountain" and ModE "iceBERG,
BURGundy"; see b̲e̲o̲r̲g̲a̲n̲ "protect" (No. 123). May be cog-
nate with Lat. f̲o̲r̲t̲i̲s̲ (Old Lat. f̲o̲r̲c̲t̲u̲s̲) "strong"
(> FORTITUDE).
Cpd.: stān-beorg. (21)

218. (ǧe-)biddan (æ, ǣ, e) (5) "BID, request, exhort,
pray"; (ǧe-)bǣdan (I) "compel, oppress."

Easy to confuse with bēodan (ēa, u, o) (2) "offer,
announce, command, foreBODE"; the two words mingled forms
in later English. Cognate are ModG bitten, Gebet, Bitte
"to request, prayer, petition." The related OE word bedu
(f.) "prayer" gives us BEAD, originally a prayer, then
the pearl-like objects with which prayers were counted:
to bid one's beads is to pray one's prayers. The relation of bǣdan to biddan is by no means certain; the
obviously similar meaning is the only real evidence of
their kinship (the verbs are baidjan and bidjan in Gothic).
(22)

219. flēon (flēah, flugon, flogen) (2) "FLEE"; flēam (m.)
"flight, escape"; [flīema (wk.m.) "escaper"]; ǧe-flīeman
(I) "put to flight, rout."

Flēon is not etym. connected with flēogan (2) "FLY (in
air)," floga "flyer," flyht "FLIGHT (in air)," but the
two groups were confused even in OE because of the likeness
of forms and sense. In ModE the verb fly can mean "pass
through the air" or "escape," but the verb now distinguishes the senses in the prets. flew and fled. Cognate
with ModG fliehen, Flucht "to flee, escape."
Cpds.: be-, ofer-flēon; here-flīema; ā-flīeman. (21)

220. frōd (adj.) "old, wise."

A chiefly poetic word, regrettably without descendents,
which means old and wise at once. Cognate with Gothic
fraþi "understanding."
Cpds.: in-, un-frōd. (21)

221. hāliǧ (adj.) "HOLY"; hālga (m.sb.wk.) "saint"; hāl
(adj.) "WHOLE, unhurt, HALE"; [hǣlan (I) "HEAL, save";
Hǣlend (m.) "Savior"; hǣl (n.) "well-being, HEALth, good
luck, (good) omen"]; hǣlo (f.) "prosperity, luck."

Health, wholeness, and sanctity are synonymous in the
Germanic langs. Our salute hail! (ModG Heil!--see sigor
No. 204) represents a wish for well-being (wes hāl!>
WASSAIL "be well"), cf. Lat. vale (not etym. related).
The w of whole is post-OE; cf. Spenser's frequent spel-
ling whot for hot (< hāt). Note the persistent long
quantity of the whole group of words. The most persist-
ent shared feature of etym. groups of words is the

initial letter (if it is a consonant)--which is fortunate
for philologists, because alphabetized lists of words
provide the first clues of family relationships.
Cpd.: un-hǣlo.

222. hām (m.) "dwelling, homestead, HOME."

Cognate with ModG Heim "home"; from a root meaning "to
rest," probably cognate with Gk. keimai, koimāō, koitos
"to lie, I put to sleep, bed," Lat. cūnae "cradle, nest."
Cpd.: hām-weorðung. (21)

223. blōd (n.) "BLOOD"; blōdiġ (adj.) "bloody";
[blōdeġian (II) "make bloody."]

Cognate with ModG Blut "blood."
Cpds.: blōd-fāg, -rēow; blōdiġ-tōþ. (20)

224. brēost (n. or f.) "BREAST."

Cognate with ModG Brust "breast." It may be distantly
related to OE byrne (No. 164), as "breast armor," but
the words are not joined here. The sense of the etymon
may be "swelling."
Cpds.: brēost-cearu, -cofa, -ġehyġd, -ġewǣde, -hord,
-nett, -weorðung, -wylm. (20)

225. ġieldan (ġeald, guldon, golden) (3) "YIELD, pay,
give."

Most common as the cpd. for-ġieldan, with a sense of "re-
paying," sometimes of requiting or exacting vengeance.
Cognate with ModG gelten "to be valid" and with mone-
tary terms (YIELD, GUILD, ModG Geld "money"). The OE
legal term wergeld is the "man-yield" (wer + ġield), the
legal price of a man, payable in cases of homicide.
Cpds.: ā-, an-, for-ġieldan. (20)

226. sār (n.) "pain, wound" (adj.) "SORE, grievous,
painful"; sāre (adv.) "sorely"; [sāriġ (adj.) "sad."]

The ModE noun SORE and the adj. SORRY (not related to OE
sorg> ModE sorrow) have both lost the idea of mortal pain
and grief of the OE words. Cognate with ModG versehren

"to wound," the group may be related to Lat. <u>saevus</u> "raging."
Cpds.: sār-līċ; līċ-sār; sārið-ferþ, -mōd. (20)

227. <u>snot(t)or</u> (adj.) "wise"; <u>snyttru</u> (wk.f.) "wisdom, skill."
Cpds.: snotor-līċe; fore-snotor; un-snyttru. (20)

Strong and Preterite-Present Verbs

This list includes all the strong and pret.-pres. verbs found in the Word-Hoard. The prefix ğe- is here ignored. The first number, in parentheses, is the frequency of the individual verb together with all its forms with prefixes. The second number is the group frequency. The principal parts are explained in the Introduction.

Strong Verbs

Class 1

(45)	46	bīdan	bād	bidon	biden	"BIDE"
(45)	52	wītan	wāt	witon	witen	"blame"
(1)	37	līðan	lāþ	lidon	liden	"go"

Class 2

(21)	63	būgan	bēag	bugon	bogen	"BOW"
(16)	117	drēogan	drēag	drugon	drogen	"undergo"
(11)	21	flēon	flēah	flugon	flogen	"FLEE"
(9)	23	čēosan	čēas	curon	coren	"CHOOSE"
(5)	23	drēosan	drēas	druron	droren	"fall"
(3)	36	lēosan	lēas	luron	loren	"LOSE"

Class 3

(82)	102	weorðan	wearþ	wurdon	worden	"become"
(36)	78	findan	fand	fundon	funden	"FIND"
(25)	37	friğnan	fræğn	frugnon	frugnen	"ask"
(19)	27	hweorfan	hwearf	hwurfon	hworfen	"turn"
(18)	38	windan	wand	wundon	wunden	"WIND"
(16)	30	bindan	band	bundon	bunden	"BIND"
(10)	38	beorgan	bearg	burgon	borgen	"protect"
(7)	150	winnan	wann	wunnon	wunnen	"fight"
(6)	20	ğieldan	ğeald	guldon	golden	"YIELD"

Class 4

(74)	90	cuman	cōm	cōmon	cumen	"COME"
(50)	140	beran	bær	bǣron	boren	"BEAR"
(44)	44	niman	nam	nāmon	numen	"take"
(1)	82	helan	hæl	hǣlon	holen	"conceal"

Class 5

(57)	78	sēon	seah	sāwon	sewen	"SEE"
(45)	64	licgan	læ̊g	lāgon	leg̊en	"LIE"
(33)	53	wrecan	wræc	wrǣcon	wrecen	"avenge"
(32)	67	sittan	sæt	sǣton	seten	"SIT"
(29)	81	g̊iefan	g̊eaf	g̊ēafon	g̊iefen	"GIVE"
(28)	37	cweðan	cwæþ	cwǣdon	cweden	"say"
(27)	28	-g̊ietan	-g̊eat	-g̊ēaton	-g̊ieten	"grasp"
(27)	30	sprecan	spræc	sprǣcon	sprecen	"SPEAK"
(17)	21	biddan	bæd	bǣdon	beden	"BID"
(12)	49	wegan	wæ̊g	wǣgon	weg̊en	"carry"
(4)	37	fricgan			fræg̊en	"ask"
(4)	39	metan	mæt	mǣton	meten	"measure"
(1)	93	wegan	wæ̊g	wǣgon	weg̊en	"fight"

Class 6

(62)	128	standan	stōd	stōdon	standen	"STAND"
(23)	26	slēan	slōg	slōgon	slæ̊gen	"strike"
(14)	69	faran	fōr	fōron	faren	"GO"
(11)	32	sciebþan	scōd	scōdon	sceaðen	"harm"
(5)	50	scieppan	scōp	scōpon	scapen	"create"
(2)	81	sacan	sōc	sōcon	sacen	"fight"

Class 7

(77)	80	healdan	hēold	hēoldon	healden	"HOLD"
(36)	101	gangan	g̊ēong	g̊ēongon	gangen	"go"
(33)	37	lǣtan	lēt	lēton	lǣten	"LET"
(25)	33	fōn	fēng	fēngon	fangen	"seize"
(24)	62	wealdan	wēold	wēoldon	wealden	"rule"
(23)	37	feallan	fēoll	fēollon	feallen	"FALL"
(17)	37	weallan	wēoll	wēollon	weallen	"surge"
(8)	57	hātan	hēt	hēton	hāten	"call"
(6)	28	weaxan	wēox	wēoxon	weaxen	"grow"
(4)	23	rǣdan	rēd	rēdon	rǣden	"counsel"
(1)	90	cnāwan	cnēow	cnēowon	cnāwen	"KNOW"
(1)	22	flōwan	flēow	flēowon	flōwen	"FLOW"

Preterite-Present Verbs

(119)	124	sculan	sceal	scealt	sceolde	"ought to"
(116)	170	magan	mæ̊g	meaht	meahte	"be able"
(46)	46	*mōtan	mōt	mōst	mōste	"may"
(34)	96	witan	wāt	wāst	wiste	"know"
		(nytan)				
(30)	61	g̊emunan	g̊eman	g̊emanst	g̊emunde	"be mindful o
(25)	90	cunnan	cann	canst	cūðe	"know (how),
(19)	43	*þurfan	þearf	þearft	þorfte	"need"
(18)	33	āgan	āh	āhst	āhte	"possess"
		(nāgan)				
(10)	41	dugan	dēag		dohte	"be good for"

Words Easy to Confuse

Like any lang., OE has many words which are homophones
or near-homophones of others, and liable to be confused.
The variety of spellings of many words only increases
the liability. From this Word-Hoard the following words
may trouble you:

1. bǣl (n.) "fire" and bealu (n.) "malice, pain, BALE."

2. ġebeorg (n.) "defense" and beorg (m.) "hill."

3. beorn (m.) "warrior, man" and bearn (n.) "child,
    son."

4. bīdan (1) "await, BIDE, remain" and ġe-bīdan (1)
    "live to experience" and biddan (5) "BID, urge,
    pray" and bǣdan (I) "compel, urge, constrain" and
    bēodan (2) "offer, announce, foreBODE."

5. cennan (I) "declare, show, make known" and cennan
    (I) "beget."

6. cunnan (pret.-pres.) "know (how)" and cunnian (II)
    "test, try, experience."

7. ealdor (or aldor) (m.) "chief, lord" and ealdor
    (aldor) (n.) "life."

8. fær (n.) "ship" and fǣr (m.) "sudden attack."

9. fāh/fāg (adj.) "hostile, outlawed" and fāg/fāh
    (adj.) "decorated, variegated, shining, stained."

10. fēran (I) "go, journey" and ġe-fēran (I) "reach"
    and faran (6, "go, FARE" and ġe-faran (6) "proceed,
    act" and ferian (I) "carry, lead, bring."

11. flēon (2) "FLEE" and flēogan (2) "FLY" (confused in
    OE).

12. frēa (wk.m.) "lord" and frēo (adj.) "free, noble"
    and frēo (f.) "lady."

13. gāst/gǣst (m.) "soul, spirit, GHOST" and ġiest/ġist/
    gæst (m.) "stranger, GUEST."

14. hēah (adj.) (wk. forms: hēan; acc. sg. m. hēanne) "HIGH" and hēan (adj.) "lowly, abject, despised."

15. herian (I) "praise" and herian (II) "plunder, assail, HARRY "

16. lēod (m.) "man" and lēode (pl.) "people" and lēod (f.) "people, nation."

17. mǣg̊ (m.) (pl. māgas) "kinsman" and magu/mago (m.) "son, young man" and maga (wk.m.) "son, young man."

18. mǣl (n.) (in cpds.) "measure" or "mark, sign" and mǣl (n.) "speech" and mǣl (n.) "time, occasion."

19. man(n) (m.) "man" and mān (n.) "crime, guilt."

20. oþþe/oþþæt (conj.) "until" and oþþe (conj.) "OR" and oþ (prep.) "up to."

21. sīþ (m.) "journey, exploit" and sīþ (comp. adv.) "later."

22. stefn (m.) "stem, prow, stern of a ship, or trunk of a tree" and stefna (wk.m.) "stem of a ship" and stefn (m.) "period, time" and stefn (f.) "voice" (ModG Stimme).

23. symbel (n.) (dat. sg. symle) "feast" and symle/symble/simble (adv.) "always."

24. syn-/sin- "ever, perpetual, great" and syn- "sinful."

25. þencan (I) "think, intend" and þyncan (I) "seem, appear."

26. wegan (5) "carry" and ge-wegan (5) "fight" and wīgan (I) "fight."

27. weorðan (3) "become, happen, be" and weorðian (II) "honor, adorn."

28. windan (3) "WIND, wave, twist" wunden (ppl. adj.) "twisted" and wund (f.) "WOUND, injury" and wund (adj.) "WOUNDed."

29. wine (m.) "friend, friendly lord" and wīn (n.) "WINE" (the beverage).

30. wītan (1) "blame, impute" and ge-wītan (1) "go, depart" and witan (pret.-pres.) "know."

31. wrecan (5) (pret. 3 sg. wræc) "drive, force, utter, avenge" and ge-wrecan (5) "avenge" and wracu (f.)

(acc. sg. <u>wræce</u>) "misery, revenge" and <u>wræc</u> (n.)
"misery, persecution, exile" and <u>reċċan</u> (I) "narrate" and <u>reċan</u>/<u>reċċan</u> (I) "care about" and
<u>rǣċan</u> (I) "REACH."

False Friends

The "Index to the Groups" shows several examples of ModE
reflexes of OE words which no longer have the same meaning,
and which frequently confuse the beginning student. Here
is a list of some which appear in this <u>Word-Hoard</u>. (Note
that the pret.-pres. verbs are special offenders.)

<u>cræftiġ</u> normally means <u>not</u> "crafty" BUT		"powerful"
<u>cunnan</u>	"can"	"know (how)"
<u>dōm</u>	"doom"	"judgement"
<u>drēam</u>	"dream"	"festivity"
<u>drēoriġ</u>	"dreary"	"bloody" or "grieving"
<u>eorl</u>	"earl"	"warrior, nobleman"
<u>grimm</u>	"grim"	"fierce"
<u>magan</u>	"may"	"can, be able"
<u>mōd</u>	"mood"	"mind, spirit"
*<u>mōtan</u>	"must"	"may, be permitted"
<u>rīċe</u>	"rich"	"powerful"
<u>sār</u>	"sore"	"grievous"
<u>scēawian</u>	"show"	"look at, examine"
<u>sculan</u>	"shall"	"ought to"
<u>sellan</u>	"sell"	"give"
<u>slēan</u>	"slay"	"strike"
<u>þynċan</u>	"think"	"seem"
<u>willan</u>	"will"	"wish"
<u>winnan</u>	"win"	"contend"
<u>wiþ</u>	"with"	"against"

KEY-WORD INDEX TO THE GROUPS

The words listed here are the head-words and a selection
of other important words from the Word-Hoard. Words
printed in capital letters are the ModE reflexes of the
etymological group, but not necessarily of the particular
form here. Items lacking words in capitals have no
obvious ModE reflex.

ac "but" 56
ǣfre "EVER" 27
æfter "AFTER" 4
ǣniġ "ANY" 17
ǣr "before" (ERE) 21
æt "AT" 40
æðele "noble" 63
āgan "OWN" 153
āglǣca "monster" 207
ān "ONE" 17
bana "slayer" (BANE) 181
be "BY" 47
bēag "ring" (BOW) 64
bealu "BALE" 170
beorg "hill" (iceBERG) 217
beorgan "protect" (BURG) 123
beorht "BRIGHT" 208
beorn "warrior" 139
beran "BEAR" 12
bīdan "BIDE" 100
biddan "BID" 218
bindan "BIND" 163
blōd "BLOOD" 223
bord "shield" (BOARD) 192
brēost "BREAST" 224
būgan "BOW" 64
burg "stronghold" (BURG) 123
byrne "corselet" (BYRNIE)
    164
čēosan "CHOOSE" 197
cræft "strength" (CRAFT) 193
cuman "COME" 32
cunnan "know" (CAN) 33
cūþ "KNOWN" 33
cweðan "say" (beQUEATH) 132
cyning "KING" 20
cynn "family" (KINdred) 20
cȳþþ "home" (KITH) 33

dæġ "DAY" 74
dǣl "share" (DEAL) 165
dēaþ "DEATH" 117
dōm "judgement" (DOOM) 26
dōn "DO" 26
drēam "festivity" (DREAM) 209
drēogan "undergo" (DREE) 19
drēoriġ "bloody" (DREARY) 198
drēosan "fall" (DREARY) 198
dryhter "lord" (DREE) 19
dugan "be good (for)"
    (DOUGHTY) 113
ēac "also" (EKE) 171
eald "OLD" 13
ealdor "life/chief" (OLD) 13
eall "ALL" 7
eard "homeland" 210
ēče "eternal" (EVER) 27
ecg "EDGE, sword" 111
ellen "valor" 108
ende "END" 199
eorl "nobleman" (EARL) 50
eorðe "EARTH" 83
fæder "FATHER" 194
fæst "firm" (FAST) 80
fāg "variegated" 140
fāh "hostile" (FEUD) 146
faran "go" (FARE) 58
feallan "FALL" 133
fela "much" (FULL) 28
fēond "enemy" (FIEND) 150
feorh "life" 37
feorr "FAR" 114
fēoa "infantry" (FIND) 48
findan "FIND" 48
flēon "FLEE" 219
flōd "FLOOD" 211
folde "earth" (FIELD) 188

folc "army" (FOLK) 84
fōn "grasp" (FANG) 154
for "FOR" 11
fōr "voyage" (FARE) 58
forma "FIRST" 11
frætwe "ornaments"(TOOL) 158
fram "FROM" 53
frēa "lord" 159
fremman "perform" (FROM) 53
frēogan "love" (FRIEND) 105
fricgan "ask" 134
friþ "peace" (FRIEND) 105
frōd "old, wise" 220
full "FULL" 28
fūs "eager" (FIND) 48
gangan "GO" 24
gār "spear" (GORE) 172
gāst/gǣst "GHOST" 212
geador "toGETHER" 162
gearu "ready" (YARE) 101
geatwe "equipment" (TOOL) 158
ġeond "throughout" (beYOND) 213
ġeong "YOUNG" 119
ġiedd "song" (GATHER) 162
ġiefan "GIVE" 43
ġieldan "YIELD" 225
ġiet "YET" 214
ġietan "grasp" (GET) 173
ġif "IF" 160
god "GOD" 103
gōd "GOOD" 14
gold "GOLD" 54
grimm "fierce" (GRIM) 141
grund "GROUND" 200
guma "man" 76
gūþ "war" 39
habban "HAVE" 22
hæleþ "warrior" 112
hāliġ "HOLY" 221
hām "HOMEstead" 222
hand "HAND" 70
hātan "call" (HIGHT) 79
hēah "HIGH" 174
healdan "HOLD" 45
heall "HALL" 42
heard "HARD" 67
heaðu- "battle-" 142
helm "HELMet" 42
heofon "HEAVEN" 185
hēr "HERE" 124
here "army" (HARBOR) 175
hīeran "HEAR" 195

hild "battle" 51
hord "HOARD" 89
hræd- "quick"(RATHER) 201
hring "RING" 166
hū "HOW" 3
hwā "WHO" 3
hweorfan "turn, go" (WHARF) 182
hwīl "WHILE" 85
hwonne "WHEN" 3
hyġe "mind" 71
īren "sword, IRON" 189
lād "course" (LEAD) 136
lǣtan "LET" 135
lāf "LEAVINGS" 30
land "LAND" 125
lang "LONG" 66
lār "LORE" 115
lāst "track" (cobbler's LAST) 115
lāþ "hostile" (LOATH) 126
lēas "without" (LESS) 143
lēod "man" 38
lēof "dear" (LOVE) 55
leoht "LIGHT" 120
lēosan "LOSE" 143
līċ "body" (LIKE) 167
licgan "LIE" 65
līefan "allow" (LOVE) 55
līf "LIFE" 30
līðan "go" (LEAD) 136
lof "renown" (LOVE) 55
lȳtel "LITTLE" 176
mǣġ "kinsman" (MAID) 34
mǣre "illustrious" 81
mæðel "council" 127
magan "can" (MAY) 5
magu "son" (MAID) 34
maniġ "MANY (a)" 90
mann "MAN" 8
māððum "treasure" 68
meaht "MIGHT" 5
metan "measure" (METE) 121
miċel "MUCH" 61
mid "with" (MIDwife) 16
mīn "MY" 41
mōd "mind" (MOOD) 25
*mōtan "may" (MUST) 102
ġe-munan "be MINDful of" 72
mynd "thought" (MIND) 72
nēah "NEAR" 177
niht "NIGHT" 151
niman "take" (NUMB) 106
nīþ "enmity" 122
nū "NOW" 59

of "OF" 4
ofer "OVER" 9
oft "OFTen" 96
oþ/oþþe "until" 104
ōðer "OTHER" 97
oþþe "OR" 155
rǣd "advice" (READ) 202
rīce "kingdom" (RICH) 147
riht "RIGHT" 203
rinc "warrior" 148
sacu "strife" (SEEK) 44
sǣ "SEA" 93
sār "grievous" (SORE) 226
sceaft "creation" (SHAPE) 92
sceaða "harmer" (SCATHING)
    161
scēawian "look at" (SHOW)
    196
scieppan "create" (SHAPE) 92
scieþþan "harm" (SCATHING) 161
sculan "must" (SHALL) 18
searu "artifice" 144
sēčan "SEEK" 44
secg "warrior" 128
secgan "SAY" 97
sefa "mind" 178
sēl "better" (SILLY) 14
sele "hall" (SALOON) 77
self "SELF" 109
sellan "give" (SELL) 137
sendan "SEND" 35
sēon "SEE" 49
sigor "victory" 204
sinc "treasure" 149
sittan "SIT" 60
slēan "strike" (SLAY) 186
sīþ "journey" (SEND) 35
sīþ "later" (SINCE) 36
snottor "wise" 227
sorg "SORROW" 129
sōþ "true" (SOOTH) 156
sprecan "SPEAK" 168
standan "STAND" 15
staðol "foundation" (STAND) 15
stōw "place" (STAND) 15
sum "SOME" 91
sunu "SON" 107
swā "SO" 2
sweord "SWORD" 78
swīþ "strong" 152
synn "SIN" 156
twā "TWO" 190
þǣr "THERE" 1
þanc "THANKS" 57

ǧe-þanc "THOUGHT" 57
þēah "alTHOUGH" 145
þeǧn "THANE" 95
þēod "nation" (DUTCH) 52
þēs "THIS" 1
þīn "THY" 179
þonne "THEN" 1
*þurfan "need" 110
þurh "THROUGH" 118
þynčan "seem" (THINK) 57
under "UNDER" 62
upp "UP" 9
ūt "OUT" 215
wæl "slaughter" (VALHALLA) 86
wǣpen "WEAPON" 157
wæter "WATER" 187
wealdan "rule" (WIELD) 69
weall "WALL" 180
weallan "surge" (WELL) 138
weard "guardian" (WARD) 82
weaxan "WAX" 171
weǧ "WAY" 94
weorc "WORK" 75
weorod "troop" 205
weorold "WORLD" 99
weorþ "WORTH" 130
weorðan "become" (WEIRD) 23
wer "man" (WEREWOLF) 99
wīd "WIDE" 116
wīǧ "war" 31
wiht "creature" (AUGHT) 191
willan "WILL" 6
windan "WIND" 131
wine "friend" (WISH) 10
winnan "fight" (WISH) 10
winter "WINTER" 206
wīs "WISE" 29
witan "know" (WIT) 29
wītan "blame" (WITNESS) 88
ǧe-wītan "go" (WIT) 88
wiþ "against" (WITH) 46
word "WORD" 73
wræc "misery, exile"
    (WRETCH) 87
wrecan "drive, avenge, utter"
    (WREAK) 87
wudu "WOOD" 216
wundor "WONDER" 183
wunian "dwell" (WISH) 10
wynn "joy" (WISH) 10
wyrd "fate" (WEIRD) 23
wyrm "serpent" (WORM) 184
ymb(e) "about" (BY) 47
ȳþ "wave" 169